LATIN AMERICA

A Cultural Outline

Stephen Clissold

Harper Colophon Books
Harper & Row, Publishers
New York

This book was originally published by Hutchinson & Co. (Publishers), Ltd., in Great Britain and is here reprinted by arrangement.

First HARPER COLOPHON edition published 1966 by
Harper & Row, Publishers, Incorporated,
49 East 33rd Street, New York, N.Y. 10016.

LIBRARY OF CONGRESS CATALOG CARD NUMBER: 66-17543

Contents

Introduction

'Our past has not yet become a real past; it is still a present which does not choose to become history.'
LEOPOLDO ZEA

Not long ago a distinguished Peruvian published a book called *Does Latin America Exist?* The title apparently did not find favour—for who likes to think that his world might be a fiction? —and in the next edition it was changed to the more grandiloquently reassuring *A Spectroscopic Examination of Latin America*. But the original choice of title is revealing. For the last century and a half, thoughtful Latin Americans have been asking much the same question. What is the nature of the society of which they find themselves a part? Is it a peripheral form of Western civilisation, a reflection, or at best an extension, of European culture? Or is it something *sui generis*, something specifically (though not in the Anglo-Saxon connotation) 'American'? Can Latin America, in short, be said to exist in anything but a geographical sense? Does it possess a mind, a personality, of its own?

The following pages will be largely concerned with this enquiry. And if the reader cannot expect to find confident answers to questions which still perplex the Latin Americans at least he may hope to learn what these questions are, how they came to be asked, and the different responses they have elicited. But first it may be worth taking a closer look at the terms in which our enquiry is framed. The twenty republics to the south of the United States range from Spanish-speaking countries as unlike each other as Mexico, Cuba or Argentina, and French-speaking, preponderantly negro Haiti, to gigantic Portuguese-speaking Brazil, a country whose distinctive problems it will be more convenient to study in a chapter apart. No wonder it has proved difficult to find a term suitable to denote all these varied countries. South America, Latin America, Ibero-America, Indo-America, Eurindia, and other names have been proposed, but none is wholly satisfactory, for each expresses but certain facets of a complex reality. 'South America' will not do, for it excludes Mexico and the Caribbean and Central American states. 'Spanish America' rules out the largest unit, Brazil. Indo-America cannot apply to countries like Argentina, Uruguay, and Costa Rica, which have virtually no Indians. 'Ibero-America' is inappropriate where the Indian heritage is stressed. Eurindia is too fanciful. We are left then with Latin America as the term most generally in use and perhaps the least unsatisfactory. How 'Latin', however, are the still numerous Quechua-speaking Indians of the Andes?

The problem of nomenclature is of more than philological interest. It leads us straight to the heart of Latin America's history and of much of its current thinking and perplexities—the violent clash between two utterly disparate worlds, followed by a long process of symbiosis, if not of synthesis. Men of the conquering race at first continued to regard themselves as Spaniards or Portuguese and to think and behave as Europeans. But the New World, with its exotic environment, its different usages, interests, and attitudes born of contact with the subject races with whom the *conquistadores* mingled their blood, inexorably modified the pattern. By the time the French and American Revolutions pointed the way to political independence, the colonists no longer felt themselves to be Spaniards or Portuguese. Exactly *what* they were was more difficult to say. 'We are mankind in microcosm', wrote Simón Bolívar. 'We possess a world of our own, bounded by vast seas, new in almost all the arts and sciences, though to some extent old in the usages of civilised society. . . . We are neither Indians nor Europeans, but something intermediate between the rightful owners of the land and the Spanish usurpers.' But even after achieving independence, Latin America was still widely regarded culturally, if no longer politically, as simply an expression of the Iberian heritage—a view which has died hard in Europe, where Latin American literature, thought, and art have traditionally been studied (if at all) as footnotes to the history of Spanish or Portuguese culture. A large proportion of the population, particularly in the Andean republics and Central America, have remained altogether unconcerned with the debate. The unassimilated Indian communities have proved alien and indifferent to the Latin American republics as they were to the Spanish Empire, subordinate to the white man's rule, but living their own lives in their own way and clinging tenaciously to ancestral tradition.

Unlike the Indian, the mixed blood or *mestizo* has been painfully conscious of his ambivalent position. Offspring of two civilisations and cultures, he was heir to neither. Feeling himself superior to the one, he was treated as an inferior by the other. The most diverse assessments have been given of his innate aptitudes. The earlier view was generally uncomplimentary in the extreme. He was described as embodying the defects of both races and the virtues of neither. The arrogance, turbulence, and verbose pretensions of the Spaniard were said to be his, coupled with the shiftiness and shallowness of the Indian. If he had negro rather than Indian blood, the mixture was considered still more tainted, for *mulatto* was frankly a term of abuse. In short, as Carlos Octavio Bunge (an Argentine of German descent) proclaimed in *Our America,* a book which enjoyed some esteem sixty years ago, the *mestizo* was a degenerate and dangerous misfit, to whom all the ills of a backward country could be ascribed. *Pueblo Enfermo* is the significant title of another book published a few years later, though here the malady is diagnosed as stemming at least in part from the adverse physical environment. But gradually a different view gained ground. The notable part played by *mestizos* in the struggle for independence and their growing importance in the life of the republics began to gain recognition. The new evaluation does not deny or decry the hybrid nature of the *mestizo* but lauds it rather as the truly original and creative principle of Latin American civilisation. Gilberto Freyre, the Brazilian social historian, developed this theme in a famous work, *Masters and Slaves,* which lays special stress on the importance of the negro element in his country's life and culture. Vasconcelos, the Mexican thinker and educationalist, proclaimed his faith that Latin America, and Brazil in particular, was destined to become the cradle of what he called the 'cosmic race', whose culture would in time spread over the whole world. Alberto Luis Sánchez, author of *Does Latin America Exist?* concludes his book with the affirmation that 'without hyperbole or oratorical metaphor, we hold in our hands the responsibility for rebuilding the culture of the world, to give shape to the New World. We have a debt to pay; not to Yesterday, but to Today and Tomorrow.'

These are high claims; is there anything in Latin America's Yesterday which holds the promise for this grand Tomorrow? What contribution have her writers and *pensadores* already made to literature and thought? The reader may be able to think of Latin American painters, architects, or musicians, but in literature he is likely to fall back on the names of an Alarcón or a Rubén Darío whose work is frequently accounted a part of Spanish letters. Latin American writing gives too often the impression of some vast miscellany, of luxuriant drafts for a fair copy which still remains to be made. Their authors have the fatal gifts of natural eloquence and exuberant imagination. They seem always in a hurry, fired with the ambition to excel in half a dozen other fields—politics, business, society, the professions—as well as letters. Brilliant improvisation comes to them more easily than the labour of pruning and perfecting. They tend to rush through successive stages of development without allowing their talent time to mature, so that, as Alfonso Reyes, one of Mexico's most distinguished writers, puts it, 'the new product resembles a dish that has been taken from the fire before it was done'. Because Latin America has arrived late at the banquet of civilisation she has been obliged to nourish herself on what others set before her, and only now is she beginning to feel the urge to prepare her own fare in her own way. In the past Latin Americans have tended to assert the individuality of their culture in terms of what it is *not*, rather than of what it is. A century and a half ago the essential was to have no part nor lot with Spain, to be other than Spanish; today it is to be other than North American, to be absolutely free of 'Yankee' tutelage, and to repudiate (even whilst accepting its material benefits) the 'American way of life'. To be anti-American seems to be the hallmark of most Latin

Americans today, as being anti-Spanish was the hallmark of an earlier generation. Anti-Americanism is not the invention of the Communists, though the latter have been quick to exploit it. The Cuba of Fidel Castro has not turned anti-American because it was Communist; it would be more true to say that it has been to some extent predisposed to Communist appeals because anti-American feeling there was particularly strong. It was in Cuba that Spanish domination lasted the longest, and the sense of national and cultural identity was consequently weakest. Until the end of the last century, to be Cuban was to feel oneself other than Spanish. Since then, when the island stood in danger of annexation by the United States, as its economy became dominated by American business and its capital converted into a pleasure ground for American tourists, to be Cuban was equated with being other than American. It was natural that Cubans, as their sense of nationhood developed, would accept as their leader one who was vehemently and eloquently anti-American, and seek as their ally the state and the social system which appeared to them most opposed to the United States. Should the influence of that power and social system prove in turn unbearably pervasive and humiliating, shall we find the Cubans seeking to assert their *cubanidad* by proving themselves to be non-Soviet and non-Communist, as they showed themselves yesterday to be non-Spanish, and show themselves today to be non-American?

In repudiating their 'Spanishness', the fathers of Latin American independence also repudiated the traditional respect for legitimacy. The Crown had been recognised as the natural source of all authority. The *Conquista* itself, though the achievement of individual adventurers, was sanctioned and consolidated by the Crown. If an individual *conquistador*, like Hernán Cortés, pulled off a conquest with little or no title to do it, he took good care to legitimise it. Even disregard of royal orders was cloaked with a fitting show of loyalty; the formula *obedezco pero no cumplo* ('I obey but do not carry out') was invoked by wary officials on receiving instructions which local conditions or vested interests might invalidate. The rulers of the new republics found themselves free of the reality or pretence of this remote control; but on what was their new authority based? On 'the will of the People'? But the people had often been divided in the struggle for independence, and different sectors now championed their own candidates for power. So the new rulers sought legitimacy in new constitutions—constitutions which they themselves made and re-made, basing them on the best models which Europe or North America could provide, and embodying the most admirable and enlightened provisions. No country had a more exemplary constitution than Bolivia, or a more lamentable record of dictatorial rule. The new constitutions were too often unrelated to the realities of the Latin American scene. They did not arise organically from the nature and traditions of the people whose affairs they were intended to regulate. The naive belief of the founders of the new republics, that they had only to discover and promulgate the perfect constitutions and good government would automatically follow, was soon seen to be a delusion. Constitutions were either ignored (*obedezco pero no cumplo*), replaced by others, or simply suspended. The founders of Latin American independence ended their lives in exile and disillusion. 'They had done no more', wrote Bolívar, 'than plough the sea.' Power was no longer exercised in the name of one unifying principle: the Spanish Crown. It had passed into the hands of anyone strong, clever, and unscrupulous enough to seize it—into the hands of the *caudillo*.

The despot is a familiar figure in all ages and lands, but the *caudillo* is his distinctively Latin American embodiment. In essence, the *caudillo* is a local phenomenon, the boss of a district who, if lucky and resolute, may become the boss of a nation which he will continue to rule in much the same arbitrary way as his private domains. If given time enough, he will consider it natural to extract a personal fortune from the nation as he does from his family estate, thereby enabling himself and his dependants to live honourably in exile when another takes over. His training in power often derives from possession of a *hacienda*, one of the great landed estates whose origins go back to the fiefs allotted to the *conquistadores* and which are still a characteristic feature of Latin American agriculture and society. He may also, less frequently, be a self-made man, having more native than European blood; *cacique*, the native term for a chieftain, is sometimes used synonymously for *caudillo*. Often he climbs to power through the Army, which he continues to use, together with the police, as the means to maintain himself in power, until he in turn is ousted by another more vigorous and cunning than himself. This follows through one of the 'revolutions' for which Latin America has become famous and which, since there is no tradition of constitutional devolution of office, serve as a mechanism for the transfer of power. Though the latter is won and wielded by the *caudillo* without regard to any real principle of legitimacy, constitutional trappings are as far as possible retained. Elections may be held and parliaments summoned. Often he may enjoy the genuine devotion and loyalty of the masses, who applaud him as their *jefe*, their *benefactor*, or their *líder máximo*. With or without this popular support, he will impose his rule with the ruthlessness so vividly described in Miguel Angel Asturias's novel *El Señor Presidente* (1946), which reflects Guatemala's experience of the twenty-two years' tyranny of the dictator Estrada Cabrera. The *caudillo* does not tolerate the existence of any independent centres of power, or any effective system of constitutional checks and balances; nor would this be expected of him by the people, who would interpret it as evidence that he is not really the strong man they wish to see as their ruler. The *caudillo* exercises power through a reliable network of kinsmen, friends, retainers, and backers, who formed the nucleus of his strength as a local boss, and who now virtually run the country, expecting and receiving due rewards for their loyalty. These personalist groupings may call themselves political parties. But parties, in the sense of bodies having a clear programme and a nation-wide democratic organisation, are rare in Latin America.

Such has been the general picture in Latin America during the last century and a half. The canvas is vast, and in places the pattern has been modified. In Uruguay, Chile, or Costa Rica, for example, the *caudillo* has latterly been little in evidence. Mexico, Bolivia, and Cuba have had revolutions which are more than palace *coups*. But where the *caudillo* motif has been strong, he also finds its counter-motif, which we may call that of the 'Man of Letters'—the man who thinks, writes poems, novels, essays, manifestoes, and stirs his fellows with an invocation to liberty and respect for human values. The most dramatic example of the confrontation between *caudillo* and a man of letters was perhaps the long duel fought between the fanatically clerical President García Moreno of Ecuador and the liberal writer Juan Montalvo, who could boast at length: 'My pen has killed him!' When, after a succession of dictators, the Venezuelan people could at last freely elect their President, their choice fell upon their most famous novelist, Rómulo Gallegos; but he was soon chased into exile. The long tyranny of Trujillo was followed by the election of a well-known Dominican writer, Juan Bosch, as President; but he too was soon ousted by a *coup*. Perhaps, to survive the rough and tumble of political life, the man of letters must himself have something of the *caudillo* about him. This was certainly the case with Sarmiento, the famous Argentine writer, who bitterly opposed the dictator Rosas and in time became President himself; for all his denunciations of the barbarity of the *gauchos* which made such dictatorships possible, Sarmiento once confessed that he was himself a *gaucho civilizado*. But whatever despotic streaks such men of letters may have in their make-up, they are of different stuff from the traditional *caudillo*. In place of the *caudillo*'s network of local and personal interests, they have their prestige as writers and the influence of their thought. They are less likely to look at national problems from a sectional point of view or to reward their henchmen at the expense of the public purse. They are expected to bring a trained intellect and high principles to bear on public affairs. The surprising thing is not that these men of letters, turned men of action—and a remarkably large number of Latin Americans do assume this double role—should sometimes prove unequal to the task, but that their people should naturally and repeatedly entrust such tasks to them. Where else in the world do states, as a matter of course, choose leading poets and essayists as their ambassadors and elect novelists as heads of state? It is this attitude which, despite the brash materialism of their cities and the selfishness of their ruling cliques, gives substance to the Latin Americans' claim that they stand for cultural and spiritual values which are too often neglected in more technically advanced countries.

Latin Americans may also point to the notable part which universities play in the life of the countries. Wherever the rule of *caudillo* or military *junta* is harshest, opposition is likely to find expression through the university, and though the government may not stop at banning political parties, gagging the Press, and jailing opponents, it will think twice before violating the hallowed principle of university autonomy. The Latin American University shares with the Church and the Army the distinction of being one of the few institutions in Latin America standing firm amidst the shifting sands of personalist policies. Although its doors have traditionally been open only to the ruling élite, who sent their sons there to be trained as lawyers, doctors, priests, and humanists, it has shown considerable capacity for self-renewal. On academic grounds it may be open to grave criticism; it is generally poorly supplied with books and equipment, its teaching staff is badly paid, and its student wastage rate appalling. Its curricula may be out of date and its research output negligible. But the university aspires to more than an academic role: it sees itself as a great civic institution, the vanguard of progressive ideas, where the student body not only acquires professional skills but, by participating in university administration and political movements, forges the new generation of national leaders.

University students form the largest, most militant, and best organised component of the 'intelligentsia' which is the chief bearer of the revolutionary impulse in Latin America. They constitute a major factor in national politics. Without the students of Havana University, for instance, it is unlikely that there would have been any Cuban Revolution, for Castro's movement was an extension to the national plane of revolutionary techniques and cadres developed in the university. Resentful of the traditional social structure which reserves positions of power and wealth to the landowning oligarchy, students have strong personal inducements for radical change. The appeal of Marxism remains strong, though in some countries it is facing the challenge of a Christian Democracy scarcely less radical and militantly 'anti-imperialist' in character. The appeal of nationalism is even stronger, though to speak of 'Latin American nationalism' has less meaning than to speak of Mexican, Argentine, or Brazilian nationalism. For the Latin American countries have been progressively differentiating themselves not only from Europe and the United States but from each other. Whilst the countries of Europe are increasingly aware of their common heritage and draw together in new forms of association, the Latin American republics are still exploring the sensation of their separate identities. The Chilean feels himself to be more Chilean, the Mexican more Mexican, than a century ago.

But even when this process of differentiation is taken into account, one may still speak of a 'Latin American Mind'. The Latin American republics spring from the same historical and cultural background and have certain basic attitudes and aspirations in common. It is still a mind in the making, marked by uncertainties and contradictions which may well intensify before they resolve themselves into the fully integrated personality. It has also the most exciting potentialities. The vast physical resources awaiting development have their counterpart in the spirit. One has the sense that the moment of mental 'take-off' may not be far off, and that startling changes may then occur. New formulas are being put forward, new models held up. 'The Latin America of today is the China of Yesterday; the China of Today is the Latin America of Tomorrow' is a 'poem' which has been given recent currency in Cuba. But most thinking Latin Americans have no wish to see their countries as another China, another Russia, another North America, or another Europe. What they wish to see is a Latin America which is truly itself, which has explored and harmonised its own diverse potentialities, rediscovered its past, and incorporated the still living structure into its personality, a Latin America which looks to others only in order to be genuinely itself. A Latin America which has, in the fullest sense of the term, acquired a mind of its own.

1
The Indian Mind

'Had my pen the gift of tears, I would write a book called *The Indian* and make the world weep.'

MONTALVO

The New World, which burst upon the gaze of the first Europeans with such startling novelty, was already, by the time-scale of human endeavour, a world of considerable antiquity. The Aztec and Inca empires encountered by the Spaniards were themselves but the latest of those waves of conquest and civilisation which had succeeded each other in certain areas of the continent since time immemorial. The Mayas of Central America had reached the apogee of their civilisation nearly a thousand years before. The magnificent embroideries found in the Paracas necropolis of coastal Peru may be five or six hundred years older. Whilst we need not go so far as those who ascribe to the ruins of Tiahuanaco, high on the Peruvian *altiplano,* an altogether fabulous antiquity as the 'cradle of American Man' and the fount of all civilisation it is certain that the life and thought of the native races had been shaped by a long and distinctive past. The newcomers from Europe were to open an entirely new chapter of American history, but the page on which they wrote it was far from blank.

The areas in which the great pre-Columbian civilisations had developed were Middle America, covering territories now part of Mexico, Guatemala, and other Central American states, and the great Andean plateau—the Bolivia, Peru, and Ecuador of today—with adjacent parts of the Pacific coast, now largely desert. In other regions, such as the highlands of Colombia, lived Indian communities already well on the path to civilisation. Other Indian tribes, such as the dread Caribs who have added the word cannibal to our language, were still in a state of savagery. These vast cultural differences were deepened by a multiplicity of tongues and dialects. Some Indian languages, such as Nahuatl in Mexico and Quechua in Peru, had become not only effective instruments of state communication but subtle and flexible media for the expression of poetry and mythology. Few Europeans succeeded in penetrating this formidable language barrier. The friars set about the task with exemplary fervour, and by adopting Quechua as the lingua franca for their missionary endeavours in Peru, they actually extended its use to areas which it had never reached under the Incas. But to learn a language well enough for practical purposes is not necessarily to command the gateway to the mind. The friars discovered this when they came to translate the Gospels. Not that Quechua lacked the necessary sophistication; on the contrary, its extremely analytical structure required the blunt Latin of the Vulgate to be refined upon in a manner fraught with theological peril.

The problem was thus not that the native mind was too primitive to accept European ideas but that it was cast in a totally different mould, for which those ideas had little or no relevance. Nor, in view of the marked differences of race, language, and cultural level amongst the natives, can we really speak of any generic 'Indian mind', except in the sense that a single mind may contain within itself varying degrees of consciousness, different and even contradictory impulses and thoughts, ranging from the most rudimentary to the highest form of which that particular mind is capable. The 'backwardness' of the Indian in relation to the European was most evident in the technological field. There was little knowledge of metallurgy (except for the working of gold and silver), few domesticated animals, no wheeled transport. Methods of recording and communicating ideas, even at their most advanced, were still nearer to picturegrams than to true writing. Yet the achievements of these primitive civilisations astonished the Spaniards as they gazed upon the teeming, well-ordered cities of Mexico, the palaces and the great temple pyramids, the intricate craftsmanship in gold, silver, jewels, and feathers, the floating gardens around the Aztec capital, the terraced fields, paved roads, and suspension bridges high in the Andes, the magnificence of the nobles, and the order and industry of the people. To those who looked further, there were miracles of artistic creation expressed in the carvings, pottery, and textiles of contemporary and bygone ages, and a traditional lore which ranged from the sophisticated abstractions of the Mayan calendar to a wealth of legend and popular poetry.

Much has been written of the vandalism of the *conquistadores* who melted down the Indians' exquisitely fashioned gold and silver works of art and consigned their sacred records to the flames. But there were also enlightened priests who devoted their lives to preserving and studying everything they could of aboriginal lore. Outstanding amongst them was the Franciscan Bernardino de Sahagún (1499–1590), whose monumental *Historia General de las Cosas de Nueva España*, compiled with the co-operation of the natives, remains an essential source for our knowledge of Mexican antiquity and the cornerstone of ethnological studies. We owe another invaluable work to an anonymous Quiché Indian who, soon after the conquest of what is now Guatemala, learned how to write his own language in European characters and noted down an account of the traditions and history of his people. Fifty years later a Spanish priest found this book in use amongst the Indians and transcribed it, adding a Spanish translation. The *Popol Vuh*, or Book of the People, was thus saved for posterity, and survives as one of the most remarkable products of the Indian mind. Though it relates the legends current amongst a single tribe, versions of these are to be found in one form or another from Mexico to the Argentine. They probably date back to the aboriginal dawn, long before the Mayas had developed their civilisation.

If the *Popol Vuh* throws little light on the decline of this civilisation, and why the great temple pyramids were in time abandoned to the jungle, it tells us much about the Mayas' beliefs regarding their own origins and the place of man in the universe. It relates the difficulties which the gods found in creating human beings, making them first out of mud, then out of wood, and only finally succeeding when they kneaded them from maize, the staple food of Central America. But even then the gods were not satisfied; they feared lest their creatures might equal them in wisdom. So 'the Heart of Heaven breathed mist into their eyes which clouded their sight, as when a mirror is breathed upon'. Thus did the first men lose their heavenly wisdom, and life became an endless grappling with the powers of nature, a struggle to placate or outwit the gods. Birds, animals, and insects join the game, for which the stakes are life and death, in a setting where poetic grandeur blends with the fantasy of the *Just-So Stories*. Much of the *Popol Vuh* is concerned with the adventures of the semi-divine twins who pit their wits against the malevolent beings known as the Lords of Xibalba. The latter force them to undergo a whole series of ordeals from which the brothers emerge victorious thanks to their courage and resourcefulness. Then they outwit their challengers in the ceremonial ball-game, in which defeat means death. Finally, after many adventures, they destroy the Lords of Xibalba by their superior magic and rise up into the sky to shed light on mankind as the sun and the moon.

Aztec bloodlust and Angst

The Mayas appear to have evolved an essentially peaceable civilisation. But its later stages show signs of a more martial outlook and the cult of human sacrifice. *Popol Vuh* alludes to the gods' wish to create men who would 'nourish and sustain them', and there are more specific references elsewhere to prisoners 'giving their breasts'. The meaning is made clear by carvings on Mayan stellae showing a victim stretched over a sacrificial stone whilst a priest stands with uplifted knife. Human sacrifice had probably been practised to a varying extent in America since the earliest times, but it was the Aztecs who developed it as the chief rite of their religion and the central feature of their civic and military life. How are we to explain this obsession with the monstrous practices of which not only the Spanish chronicles but the Aztec records provide such overwhelming evidence? And how can we reconcile it with the co-existence of admirable and totally inconsistent features of life and thought, as revealed in the fine Nahuatl poetry which the researches and translations of Angel María Garibay and other scholars have now rendered accessible to us? The answer seems to be that, before the coming of the Aztecs, a great civilisation had flourished, based probably on Teotihuacán, 'the City of the Gods', whose vast ruins, some thirty miles from Mexico City, have only recently been excavated. The Aztecs first appear as one of the savage tribes roaming the lands to the north of the marshy lake where they settled and built their home, both assimilating the old culture and perverting its tenets into an instrument for the extension of their military and political power.

The man whose ruthless genius formulated the ideology which both justified and facilitated the Aztecs' rapid rise was Tlacaélel, nephew and chief counsellor of Itzcoátl, a predecessor of Montezuma. Refusing kingly office for himself, Tlacaélel spurred on his people to overcome their more advanced neighbours and then set about reforming their army, judicial system, commerce, and court administration. The skills of the civilised Toltec predecessors were quickly assimilated. Tlacaélel then had the records revised to depict the newcomers as their legitimate heirs, and incorporated the Aztec gods into the Toltec pantheon, securing for the bloodthirsty tribal war-god Huitzilopochtli equal status with Tezcatlipoca and the beneficent plumed serpent Quetzalcoatl. The Mexican cosmogony envisaged time as a series of ages or 'suns', each destined to end in a natural cataclysm. The world was now in its fifth 'sun', which could only be sustained in its course by the most precious of all human offerings—the blood of human hearts. It was the proud mission of the Aztec warrior race to procure this constant nourishment, subjugating and conquering the surrounding tribes and carrying off their warriors for the honour of sacrifice. Warfare, in this mystic yet barbaric creed, was thus justified as the expression of cosmic piety, and the expansion of the Aztec state as the service due to the ever-thirsty gods.

This horrific vision of the world, despite the brilliant temporal rewards it brought to its devotees until they in turn went down before the Spaniards, was not shared everywhere in ancient Mexico. Many still held to the ancient gods, though obsessed with a sense of the transitoriness and futility of human life, from which these gods seemed to have turned away their face. 'We, Thy friends, are but a flower in Thy sight that is left to wither. Thou dost break us in pieces like an emerald, blot us out as it were a painting. We must all away to the region of the dead, the common abode of our perdition. What are we to Thee, Oh God? For this I weep, Oh Giver of Life, that Thou dost grow weary. The jade is shattered, the quetzal plume rent. Thou makest a mock of us, and we exist no more.' Nowhere is this sense of doom, of death lurking in the fulness of life, more poignantly expressed than in the poetry of Nezahualcoyotl, King of Texcoco, the city-state first reluctantly allied to the Aztecs and later swallowed up by them. We know a good deal about this monarch from the pious stories of a *mestizo* chronicler who claimed descent from him; how he ruled his people with justice and loving-kindness, imposing the death-penalty for drunkenness, but prodigal in good deeds towards his needy subjects; how he delighted in flower-gardens and aviaries, and raised a temple, bereft of any image, to the Unknown God; how, in the midst of his grandeur and his pleasures, he would be overwhelmed by a sense of the vanity of human life, of the gods betrayed and betraying:

> All the earth is a grave and nothing escapes it;
> Nothing is so perfect that it does not descend to the tomb.
> Rivers, rivulets, fountains and waters flow,

But never return to their joyful beginnings;
Anxiously they hasten on to the vast realms of the rain god.
As they widen their banks, they also fashion
The sad urn of their burial.
Filled are the bowels of the earth with pestilential dust
Once flesh and bone, once animate bodies of men
Who sat upon thrones, decided cases, presided in council,
Commanded armies, conquered provinces, possessed treasures, destroyed temples.
Exulted in their pride, majesty, fortune, praise and power.
Vanished are these glories, just as the fearful smoke vanishes
That belches forth from the infernal fires of Popocatépetl.
Nothing recalls them but the written page.

For all its intensity and curiously modern ring, this pessimism was not entirely unrelieved. The poetry of ancient Mexico, in which we hear the accents of the Waste Land blended with those of Omar Khayyám, turns repeatedly to the solace of 'flowers and song'. But these flowers and song are more than the expression of an empty epicureanism; they symbolise the power of poetry and art by which some glimmering of the divine reality behind the transitoriness of human life can be discerned.

Inca 'socialism' and poetry

The Incas, like the Aztecs, were cut off before their civilisation had reached its full flowering. They too were a race of warriors and worshippers of the sun, though their temples glittered with gold and silver in place of the obsidian knives and piled skulls of Middle America's sacrificial pyramids. They too had raised their empire on the ruins of more ancient civilisations, whose vanished life we can conjecture only from the designs on the textiles miraculously preserved in the dry sand of their burial grounds, and from the faces, figures, and intimate scenes into which their matchless pottery was fashioned. The genius of the Incas was, above all, for social organisation. Their empire, in which each community, family, and individual had his own place and received and contributed his appointed share, extended by means of an admirable system of roads and staging-posts over hundreds of miles of intractable highland. It has often been described as 'Socialist' or 'Communist'. It was certainly a system which inculcated habits of order and submissiveness which, after the ruling Inca caste had been destroyed, continued under the Spanish dispensation and indeed—though sometimes flaring into revolt or degenerating into apathy—down to the present day.

The Incas were strangers to the art of writing, though recent research suggests that a form of rebus- or proto-writing may not have been unknown to them. But their characteristic means of recording and communicating was the *quipu*, a cord to which coloured strings and variously placed knots was attached. A special group of learned men or *amautas* existed to interpret them. *Quipus* were primarily used for the statistical recording of population figures, tribute dues, agricultural produce, and the like. They may also have served as a mnemonic device for commemorating historical events and traditions. Some scholars go so far as to claim that the *quipus* served as a depository for the laws, religion, and poetry of the Indians. Quechua, the lingua franca of the empire, was an expressive medium for poetry. Much of this consisted of pious invocations, such as the following prayer to Pachacamac, whose cult was practised in the arid coastal regions:

Pity my tears,
Pity my anguish.
The most distressed
Of thy children,
The most needy
Of thy servants,
Implores thee with tears.
Grant the miracle
Of thy waters,
Grant the gift of thy rain,
To this unfortunate man,
This vassal,
Whom Thou dost command.

Some of the Spanish missionaries saw in the Pachacamac to whom such prayers were addressed a groping towards the God of the Christians. Even more striking was the cult of Viracocha the Creator, whose veneration by the ruling Inca caste supplemented the rites of sun worship prescribed as the state religion. The hymns to this Supreme Being breathe a spirit of genuine adoration and wonder:

Oh Viracocha! Root of all being,
God ever near,
Lord of shining apparel,
God who dost rule and preserve,
Who createst by merely commanding
'Be thou a man,
Be thou a woman,'
Where dost Thou hide Thyself?
Beyond the world,

Within the world?
In the midst of the clouds,
Or in the midst of shadows?
Hear me,
Answer me,
Grant that I may live
For many days,
Until my hair turns white with age,
Raise me up,
Take me in Thy arms,
And in my weariness
Help me,
Wherever Thou mayest be,
Father Viracocha.

Had the Indian mind then been vouchsafed some foreknowledge of the full Christian revelation brought by the priests to the New World? Could the ancestral beliefs of the Indians blossom in a true fusion of cultures and faiths, deepening the fusion of races which was beginning to take place? In Mexico this was clearly impossible. Nezahualcoyotl's 'Unknown God' had succumbed to the ferocious Huitzilopochtli when the Kingdom of Texcoco went down before the Aztecs; the gods of the latter were, in Spanish eyes, no more than devils whose blood-clotted temples had to be destroyed and abhorrent rites rooted out. But in Peru the confrontation of differing faiths did not seem so irreconcilable. The Church, in its first missionary impulse, did much to bridge the gulf between conquered and conquerors. The Indians could sing their old songs, set to new Christian words, in the churches which soon rose on the sites of the old temples. They could take part too in the great pageants and dramatisations which the priests devised, in the tradition of the medieval mystery plays and Spain's *autos sacramentales*, for the inculcation of the Christian truths. These plays were composed in the Quechua and Aymara tongues, sometimes by *mestizo* authors, and a few have come down to us. The new art form won great popularity, for it was rooted in a vigorous native dramatic tradition. 'The Amautas composed both tragedies and comedies, which were represented before the Inca and his court on solemn occasions', a *mestizo* writer tells us. 'The subject matter of the tragedies related to military deeds and victories of olden times, whilst the comedies treated of rustic or familiar household themes.'

One drama in this secular Quechua tradition has recently come to light in Bolivia. It relates the fate of the Inca Atahualpa, and ends—with scant regard for historical accuracy—by portraying Pizarro, his murderer, at the court of the King of Spain, where he falls down dead at his royal master's stern rebuke. This curious but moving native account of the national tragedy may have been composed not many years after the Conquest, and was performed at local fiestas down to the present century.

A more famous and polished example of Quechua drama is *Ollontay*. This work shows traces of Spanish cultural influence, and dates back, in its present form, only to the eighteenth century, when it appears to have been re-cast by a Spanish priest. It tells the story of a young warrior, not of the blood royal, who conceives a passion for an Inca princess. His suit scornfully rejected by the Inca, Ollontay raises a rebellion, seizes the fortress subsequently known as Ollontay Tampu, but is finally captured by trickery and brought before the new Inca, the famous Tupac Yupanqui. As he is being led away to execution, the magnanimous Inca pardons him, and he is united in marriage to the princess. This somewhat banal romantic story is enlivened with passages of humorous dialogue, and with exotic touches provided by the High Priest's divination of the future, a scene in the Temple of the Virgins, and a love message sent by *quipu*. The play also contains poems of rare lyrical quality, evoking the imagery of the Song of Songs.

Why has drama written in native languages and on native themes not continued to thrive in Peru? The reason is on record. *Ollontay*, we know, was performed shortly before 1781 in the presence of a local notable called José Gabriel Condorcanqui who, in that year, assumed the style of Tupac Amaru II, and rose in revolt against the Spaniards in a vain attempt to restore the throne of the Incas. After the stern repression of this rising the Spaniards forbade 'the representation of dramas as well as other festivals which the Indians celebrate in memory of their Incas'. A similar ban was also imposed, for the same reason, on the most famous literary monument to be composed in memory of the vanquished race—the *Comentarios Reales* of the Inca Garcilaso de la Vega.

Indians and Spaniards

Garcilaso de la Vega (1539–1616) was the son of one of the *conquistadores* of Peru and of an Indian princess. Brought up in Cuzco amongst the vestiges of imperial greatness and nourished with the tales and legends of Inca glory, he was nevertheless proud of his Spanish descent and chose to live in Europe, serving in the Spanish Army and devoting the rest of his life largely to letters. 'Feeling myself under obligation to two races,' he wrote, 'since I am the son of a Spanish father and an Indian mother', he composed his account of 'the origins of the Inca kings, their ancient customs, their idolatry and conquest, their laws and order of government both in peace and war'. His history of the Incas and of their conquest by the Spaniards is thus conceived 'not only for the honour and renown of the Spanish nation which has accomplished such great things in the New World, but no less for that of the Indians . . . for they too appear worthy of the same praise'. Too young to have been himself an eyewitness of the dramatic events he describes, Garcilaso writes with the authority of his childhood familiarity with the Peruvian background. Mellowed by time and distance, his scenes are evoked with gentle and poetic melancholy and depicted with the urbane grace of a mind steeped in renaissance humanism. His Indians are idealised figures, ancestors of the noble savages which were to make so powerful an appeal to the romantic imagination of a later generation.

For all its exotic fascination, the world that Garcilaso shows us is not that of the Indians themselves but a European reflection of that world. To find an authentic expression of the Indian mind we must turn to one whose work scarcely ranks as literature at all, for the adoption of literary forms, as we know them, implies in itself a certain alienation from the Indian spirit. Huamán Poma de Ayala (?1526–?1614) was a full-blooded Peruvian Indian who learned just enough Spanish to compose an extraordinary work, interlarded with Quechua and copiously illustrated by his own naive but vivid sketches, describing the traditional way of life and institutions of the Indians and their sufferings under the misgovernment of the Spaniards. Of his *Nueva Coronica y Buen Gobierno*, which took him nearly thirty years to compile and which had to wait more than three centuries for publication, Huamán Poma wrote that 'some will weep, others laugh, others curse, others will commend him to God, others from rage will want to destroy the book: a few will want to have it in their hands'. All anthropologists, scholars, and well-wishers of the Indians will be amongst the latter, for Huamán Poma's work has been described by one authority as 'the most remarkable as well as the most interesting production of native genius that has come down to our time'.

It is significant that when Huamán Poma had completed his work he presented it to the officials in Lima with the request that it should be sent to Spain for the information of the King. It is equally characteristic that both he and the Inca Garcilaso should be devout Catholics; Huamán Poma attempts to find a place for his country within the framework of biblical history by depicting the llama amongst the other animals in Noah's ark and relating tales of St Bartholomew's alleged missionary journey to the New World. Crown and Church were the two powers which stood for the defence of the Indians against the rapacity of the conquerors. The Crown, by insisting that the Indians were its subjects and not its slaves (as some of the conquerors would have had them be), and the Church, by substituting a new faith for the gods that had been overthrown, offered them a status in the alien society into which they had been so violently thrust. Though inferior, it was nevertheless a status; and that was of vital consequence, for the old societies under which they had lived were theocratic and military, and once the native priesthoods and warrior castes were annihilated, the Indians were left in utter disintegration. The Crown stepped in with a system which, in theory, reconciled the rewards of the conquerors with the needs of the conquered. The former were 'entrusted' (*encomendado*) with the physical protection of the Indians, and with seeing to their conversion and civilisation. The Indians, in return, were to serve the masters of their *encomiendas*. Clearly, the system was open to great abuse. The conquerors took their civilising duties lightly. The *encomiendas* turned into hereditary estates, with the Indians living on them in forced labour. Worse still was the lot of those Indians required to labour in the mines. Only where the Church herself took the Indians directly beneath her paternal care, as in the famous Jesuit settlements in Paraguay, could the Indians lead a secure and reasonably contented life.

The Crown also endeavoured to protect the Indians through permitting them to live on in their traditional communities. These *ayllus*, as they were called in Peru, were the shell within which the Indians retreated in order to preserve what they could of their familiar values and way of life. The Indians' withdrawal was both physical and psychological. But though the bodies of the Indians might be forced to do the bidding of their masters in field or mine, their mind remained sealed off behind a wall of distrust, resentment, and repudiation of the new world of the white man. To the latter they appeared indolent, treacherous, and incurably backward. Franz Tamayo, the Bolivian poet who was himself partly of native stock, described the Indian as 'a soul turned in upon itself; this shutting away of mind and feeling results in a kind of failure to assimilate things and ideas which come from outside'. Yet despite this mental alienation, he believed that 'all that is strongest, all that is morally best in Bolivia is the Indian'.

The Indians since independence

Indifferent to the passions and aspirations which stirred the white man's world, the Indians played only a passive part in the struggle for independence from Spain. They either held aloof from the fighting, or else followed their local *caudillo* on whichever side he happened to be. The 'Spanish' armies which held out longest against the 'patriot' forces of San Martín and Bolívar were composed mostly of Indian conscripts. Miranda might place before Pitt his exotic proposals for a South American House of Commons under a constitutional Inca monarchy, and Bolívar address the enthusiastic señoritas of Arequipa as 'Virgins of the Sun', vowing that the army of liberation would strike off the fetters forged by Pizarro for the sons of Manco Capac, while the Ecuadorean poet José Joaquín de Olmedo (1780–1847) might conjure up the shade of the last Inca to add lustre to his ode in honour of the *Victoria de Junín*, but the Indians showed little interest in gaining independence from Spain nor did they benefit from its achievement.

The idealists who framed the new constitutions believed that the Indians could be integrated into the life of the republics simply by declaring the equality of all men. There were to be Mexicans, Peruvians, Bolivians; but no Indians and whites. The special status accorded to the Indians and to their communities was abolished as discriminatory and degrading. But however well meaning the Liberal measures of emancipation may have been, they often led to a deterioration of the Indians' lot and a deepening of their isolation. The niceties of law were incomprehensible to illiterate natives who now found themselves exposed to exploitation by unscrupulous landowners greedy to enlarge their estates at the expense of the Indian communities. Forced to find money for the new taxes, the peons had still to give their service and became more than ever subordinate to the *patrón* who paid their wages and allowed them to run up debts in his store.

The gulf which separated Indian from non-Indian was more absolute than ever. To cross it there was only one way—to cease being an Indian. The Indian question in Latin America can indeed be regarded less as a racial than a cultural, economic and social one. An Indian is really one who clings to his ancestral traits and values in a non-Indian society. Once he discards these and adopts others, learns Spanish, and acquires money, he ceases to be considered an Indian and is reckoned amongst the *gente de razón*, the 'civilised people'. A non-white who fulfilled these requirements could even secure formal recognition of his changed status by obtaining from the authorities a certificate confirming that he should be 'considered white'. The 'integration' of the Indians really implies their assimilation. The Liberals who believed they were offering the natives salvation offered it to them as individuals, not as a race. Some even declared their conviction that the native races did not deserve to survive. 'The Indian is useless', was the view advance by the Bolivian Gabriel René Moreno. 'But by some monstrous deformity, the Indian is indeed a living force in Bolivia, a passive, inert mass, a stone blocking the viscera of the social organism. . . . Let the Indian and the *mestizo*, those two archaic agents, one of them Incaic and the other colonial, vanish as soon as possible; let them be stamped out by European immigration.'

The Indianist novel

Such was the view of a racist, impressed by the material prosperity brought to the Argentine by the flood of European immigrants who were displacing the savages of the *pampa*. But there was also another current of thought, literary and romantic in its inspiration, which exalted the Indians as the first innocent victims of the Spain whose yoke had now at last been cast off. It was an artificial and sentimental cult, in which we hear again the gentle, elegaic tones of the Inca Garcilaso de la Vega. It found expression in poetry, and, particularly, in *indigenista* novels whose heroes are embodiments of Rousseau's 'noble savages' or of the romantic figures moving through the pages of Marmontel, Bernardin de Saint-Pierre, and, above all, of Chateaubriand. Little attempt was made to study the models still living under the authors' eyes. It is revealing that one of most famous of these tales, Manuel Galván's *Enriquillo* (1878), was written in the island of Santo Domingo, where the Indians were long since extinct. The hero who gives his name to this book is a historical personage—an Indian chieftain who accepted baptism and the Spanish mode of life, but was driven to revolt by the injustices committed by the *conquistadores*, and maintained a heroic resistance until receiving the pardon and renewed favour of the King.

Another celebrated Indianist novel was *Cumandá* (1871), written by Juan León de Mera. The author was an Ecuadorean, and he tells us in his preface that it is based on the story told him by an English traveller who could vouch for its truth. Cumandá is a maiden of the forests who falls in love with a white youth, Carlos, whose life she saves no less than three times from the perils of nature and the malice of the Indians, finally at the cost of her own. The heroine is later discovered to be no other than Carlos' own sister, who had been carried off as a small child by the Indians and brought up as one of themselves. This romantic tale, told against the majestic background of the equatorial forest, had many imitators; it also sounds, in appealing to 'civilised society' to recognise responsibility for its primitive brothers, a note which was soon to swell into a chorus of social protest. The theme was taken up in Peru by Clorinda Matto de Turner, the hero and heroine of whose *Aves sin Nido* (1889) discover to their distress that they are both the offspring of the same licentious village priest, and in Bolivia by Alcides Arguedas in his *Raza de Bronce* (1919).

The 'bronze race' as seen by this gifted Bolivian author is not the 'passive, inert mass' whose speedy disappearance we have heard demanded in the name of progress by his educated compatriot. It is the primitive folk toiling on the great estates, often driven to revolt by the callous brutality of their owners. These are no 'noble savages' who look back with nostalgic pride to the glories of the Incas; history, for them, is no more than 'one huge stain of mud and blood', and their only ambition is to be left in peace to eke out the same wretched existence as their fathers before them. They have been brutalised by the harsh conditions of the *altiplano* and the centuries of oppression, for 'the white man, for more than four centuries, has lived only at the expense of the Indian, exploiting him, robbing him, putting him to bleed and sweat in his service. And if the Indian hates and mistrusts him, and does everything humanly possible to cause him harm, it is because he has imbibed with his mother's milk the knowledge that the white man is his natural enemy.' What power can break through this impasse? Can education, perhaps, be the Indian's salvation? 'The day when the Indian gets a schoolmaster', declares the *patrón*, 'life will become impossible for us in these parts. Woe the day when these two million Indians learn to read, handle the law-books, edit newspapers! They will do away with our estates and become the masters.' But the Indians, suspicious of all things and all men, look even upon education with distrust. 'There must be some foul poison about letters,' one Indian is made to observe, 'for whenever one of us learns to read, he turns against his own flesh and blood and uses his knowledge to exploit us too.'

This passage is revealing on several scores. It shows the difficulties facing those who believe that the school offers the gateway to a better life for the Indian. It also reminds us that even the best novels on Indian life are no more than so many interpretations of the Indian mind; it is not the Indian mind itself which speaks through them. They comprise what is rightly known as *literatura indigenista* not *literatura indígena.* With the possible exception of the Peruvian José María Arguedas (1913–), author of the powerful novel *Los Ríos Profundos,* their authors cannot be said to speak with an authentically Indian voice. For no sooner does an Indian become literate than his fellows feel him to be no longer one of themselves. The *indigenista* may convince and move us, but can we be sure that his reading of the native mind rings true? His work may tend, as in the earliest examples of the genre, towards idealisation and stylisation. Or, if the author's emotion is too fierce and politically motivated, it may be distorted into caricature. Both these tendencies may be seen respectively in the work of two leading contemporary exponents of the Indianist novel: the Peruvian Ciro Alegría (1908–), and the Ecuadorean Jorge Icaza (1902–).

The best known, and probably the best written, of Alegría's novels is *El Mundo es Ancho y Ajeno* (1941), which describes the life of an Indian community and its destruction at the hands of a grasping landowner. We first see the community through the eyes of its Indian headman, Rosendo Maqui—or is it simply through the eyes of its sympathetic but non-Indian author?—as he gazes and meditates on it one afternoon; 'it was a delight to see the gay picture the village made, and still more delightful to live there. What does civilisation know? . . .

The villagers of Rumi were contented with their lot.' But Don Alvaro, the local landowner, covets their land, and with the help of a crooked lawyer has them evicted. Some, in desperation, turn bandits, others are forced to toil as rubber-gatherers in the jungle, the rest attempt to rebuild what is left of the community elsewhere. But all is in vain; the malevolence and cupidity of the landowner inexorably pursue them and the remnants of the community are finally wiped out. It is this community, prototype of countless others which have met a like fate in the *altiplano*, that is the protagonist of the novel. Rumi is destroyed for ever; but we are left with the conviction that the virtues of the score or so of Indian men and women whose life-story is here told—their dignity, patient kindness, decency, and courage—are imperishable and must prove the ultimate salvation of their race.

The subject of Icaza's novel is also the destruction of an Indian community. In *Huasipungo* (1934) (a Quechua word for the tiny plot of land which the Indians are allowed to work in return for their forced labour on the estate) a landowner sells his property to a foreign company who wish to set up a timber mill. The Indians are no longer needed; after being forced to build a road they are hounded from the land of which they feel themselves to be a part, and are mercilessly destroyed by an unholy alliance between landowner, priest, political boss, and *gringo* capitalist. It is a dark, brutal story, brutally told. The characters are not individuals but dehumanised symbols of evil and violence. The book does not aim at giving us a sympathetic insight into the Indian mind but rather at inspiring disgust and horror for those who traditionally exploit them. We are wrenched from the world of literature into that of crude political cartoon.

The limitations of such a socio-political approach are apparent. The Indian sees life in terms which are at once more primitive and more complex than those postulated by social realism; his reality, despite the intrusions of twentieth-century pressures, is still largely compounded of myth and magic. To treat of it one needs to be poet and anthropologist as well as novelist and politician. Such a writer is Miguel Ángel Asturias (1899–) whose *Hombres de Maíz* (1949) portrays the Indians of Guatemala as still moving in the legendary world of *Popol Vuh*. True descendants of the 'men of maize' who, according to their mythology, were the first true human beings to be created by the gods, they still feel themselves to be a part of the mystic body of nature and engage in desperate struggle against those who profane and exploit nature by growing crops merely for commercial profit. It is a dense, confusing, fantastic world, whose protagonists are not only the Indians and their enemies of the unholy alliance, but also witch-doctors, rocks charged with magical powers, and humans transmogrified into animals.

The Indian problem in Peruvian political thought

Is then the cleavage between Indian and White absolute, the enmity between them quite irreconcilable? This question began to be asked with a new urgency in Peru around the turn of the present century, after the country, once so powerful and glorious, had suffered a humiliating defeat at the hands of a Chilean expeditionary force. González Prada (1848–1918), the leading Peruvian writer of the day, believed that his country's decadence was due to the fact that it had not yet acquired a real sense of nationality; the two separate worlds of oppressor and oppressed, white man and Indian, still lived on side by side in mutual hostility and incomprehension. 'The condition of the Indian can be improved in two ways', he wrote. 'Either the heart of the oppressor is softened to the point of recognising the rights of the oppressed, or else the oppressed should become stout-hearted enough to turn against the oppressors.' History has shown few signs of the former occurring, so he held that 'the Indian should not be exhorted to humility and resignation but to pride and rebellion'.

González Prada was a prophet, not a political organiser; he made little attempt to give practical effect to the revolutionary creed which he advocated. Nor did he work out a detailed programme for the social and political transformation which he believed to be necessary. This was left to a younger *mestizo* compatriot—José Carlos Mariátegui (1895–1930). Mariátegui was converted to Marxism whilst studying in Europe, and returned determined to apply a searching Marxist analysis to the problems of his own country. His ideas were expressed in a review which he called *Amauta* (the name by which the Inca sages had been known) and were later collected in book form under the title of *Siete Ensayos de Interpretación de la Realidad Peruana* (1928). 'We are a country where natives and *conquistadores* still go on living cheek by jowl, without intermingling, without understanding each other', he wrote, taking up González Prada's thesis. Far from the heart of the oppressor ever being softened towards the Indians, a whole system of vested interests bolstered his power: the judiciary and the legislature, controlled by members of the landowning oligarchy, the police, and the Army, which carried out their bidding, the *mestizo* foremen who worked in their interest, the school which reflected the ethos of their society. The only way to weaken the grip of the landowner was to cut at the root of his power—the ownership of land. Mariátegui does not advocate a land reform on liberal lines. This had already been tried at times, and had led not to the creation of a class of Indian small-holders, but to the aggrandisement of the landowners themselves. Mariátegui believed that the Indian community should be strengthened at the expense of the landowner. The *ayllu*, he maintained, though weakened by misguided liberal legislation, was still a living force. Even where the communities were officially disbanded 'there still persist robust and tenacious habits of co-operation and solidarity which are the empirical expression of a communist spirit'. Mariátegui does not of course equate the primitive agrarian communism of the Incas with the Communism of Marx and Engels, nor does he advocate, in so many words, the conversion of the large estates into collective farms. But he does suggest that the Indians' strong instinct for communal action should be taken into account in working out the future transformation of his country which he believed to be inevitable. He gives several examples of *ayllus* which have proved remarkably successful in adopting new techniques, even showing greater productivity than the *hacienda* where farming conditions were more favourable, thus giving the lie to the alleged congenital inferiority of the Indians. Mariátegui, in short, extols the *ayllu* 'not on abstract principles of justice nor for sentimental traditional reasons, but on sound practical and economic grounds'.

Mariátegui died young, after founding a political group which was to become the Peruvian Communist Party. But the Communists (some of whom suspected that Mariátegui's ideas smacked of populism) were overshadowed in the next decade or so in Peru by another revolutionary movement; the *Alianza Popular Revolucionaria Americana* (APRA). Although APRA's founder, Haya de la Torre, built up his following primarily amongst students and labour, and did not include any specifically Indianist plank in his original platform, he later became a vigorous champion of the concept of 'Indo-America'. 'The new revolution in our America', he declared, 'will be Indian in its basis and character, and will express itself consciously or subconsciously in the economic and social regeneration of the native.' It was not APRA, however, but Fernando Belaunde Terry's *Acción Popular* party which, in the early sixties, was returned to power with a programme invoking the example of the Incas in such fields as state planning, communal co-operation, and road construction. These ideas were interestingly developed in Belaunde's *La Conquista del Peru por los Peruanos* (1959) before his election to the presidency of the Republic. That Peru should seek inspiration in her pre-Columbian past and find ways of preserving what she can of her Indian heritage and of incorporating her Indian population into the life of the nation has thus now been recognised by thinkers of many different views. Young people from the cities are now beginning to explore for themselves the realities of the Indian world in much the same way as the *narodnik* intelligentsia of pre-revolutionary Russia concerned themselves with the conditions of their peasantry.

The Indian in the Mexican Revolution

If Peru is still searching for a solution to her Indian problem, Mexico can claim to have had both a revolution and, to some extent, an Indian resurgence. Mexican society had been similar to that of Peru, though a larger proportion of the great estates were held by the Church or by foreigners. The status of the Mexican Indians was no less miserable, in spite of the larger measure of racial fusion which had taken place. In its early stages, the Mexican Revolution had not been animated by any particular vindication of Indian rights, but, as it developed, a powerful movement for the occupation of the great estates arose amongst the Indians themselves. By the time the Revolution had triumphed it had taken on a marked Indianist character. The old ruling and landed class, heirs to the Spanish conquerors, had been forced to yield to the *mestizo* and Indian substrata. The Revolution, it was proclaimed, had at last righted the wrongs suffered by the indigenous population following the Spanish conquest and four centuries of white domination.

The economic basis for the land reform which lay at the heart of the Mexican Revolution was the establishment, or re-establishment, of *ejidos*. Similar in some respects to the Peruvian *ayllu*, these units permitted the co-operative holding or working of land amongst the Indians, which seemed to accord better both with their economic needs and with their traditional mentality than a purely individualist system. At the same time, a vigorous movement was launched to raise the Indian from his educational and technical backwardness and to draw him fully into the life of the nation by the construction of rural schools which would also serve as nuclei for the general advance of their community in hygiene, literacy, agrarian skills, and political awareness. A brilliant school of painters, headed by Rivera, Orozco, and Siqueiros, covered the walls of public buildings in the cities with compelling murals exalting the glories of Mexico's pre-Columbian past and the eventual triumph of the long oppressed native races. Cuauhtémoc, the last of the Aztec princes, was taken to symbolise the true spirit of Mexico, where one might search in vain for a single statue commemorating the achievement of the great Hernán Cortés. The enhanced importance of the Indian element is illustrated by the Mexican population figures. Though the census of 1921 showed a slight drop in total population as a result of the years of revolutionary turmoil, the number of persons classified as Indians is placed at over four million as compared with little more than a million and a half in 1910. To belong to the native race is no longer a stigma to be disguised. Yet the rehabilitation of the Mexican Indian, striking though it has been, is still far from complete. There are still Indian communities in Mexico sunk in poverty and backwardness and aloof from the life of the nation. The complexity of reversing century-old socio-political processes and creating a new mentality is reflected in recent Mexican literature. Gregorio López y Fuentes' novel *El Indio* (1935), which describes the misery brought upon an Indian community by a band of white men in search of gold, the ensuing disasters of witchcraft, epidemics, divisions, forced labour, and the first glimmerings of hope brought by the Revolution, ends on a note of caution: the Indians gaze out over the highway which may lead them to what the whites call civilisation, still unsure whether the promise of a better life is real. In another remarkable novel, *Balun Canan* (1957) by Rosario Castellanos, we see that passing of the old order, through the eyes of a child, daughter of a dispossessed landowner; can these Indians, enigmatic and vengeful, become the stuff of a better social order? We are again left with the strong impression that such insights as we get into the Indian mind are inevitably coloured by their author's views. How can we hear the authentic voice of the Indian himself?

One such rare revelation comes to us through a work—whether we should classify it as novel, biography, or anthropological study is hard to say—by Ricardo Pozas (1910–). *Juan Pérez Jolote* (1952) tells the story of a Tzotzil-speaking

Indian from Mexico's province of Chiapas, near the Guatemalan border. We see him caught up in the revolutionary armies, where he picks up Spanish and *mestizo* ways. He then returns to his village but is regarded there as a foreigner. He has to win re-acceptance into Indian life, discarding his town clothes, re-learning the natives' language, entering anew into their lore and the cycle of their fiestas and office-holding. The life of Juan Pérez Jolote shows that being 'Indian' is basically less a matter of race than of cultural and social status. His experience reveals the process of aculturation which has been going on since the Spaniards set foot in America. But how superficial and precarious the process may be we learn from the less usual feature of Juan's story; his decision to revert to his ancestral ways and to resume his place in Indian society. So the course of assimilation is reversed; Juan once again becomes an Indian, retaining nothing of the white man's culture save a smattering of his language, and resuming the traditional values of his people, whose respect is his highest prize and semi-ritual intoxication the hallmark of social standing, and where the ancient pagan beliefs still rule men's lives beneath the accretions of Catholicism.

The Indian's place in the modern world

The place which the Indian is willing and able to take in the modern world thus remains far from clear. Some observers still hold the traditional view of his innate incapacity for western civilisation and characterise his mentality as, in the words of Salvador de Madariaga, 'a kind of listlessness, a forlorn, passive, silent, sullen state, relieved only by bouts of drunkenness, or if provoked, by the excitement of war'. Others who have known the Indian long and intimately speak of his qualities in the warmest terms; he is hard-working, patient, honest and shrewd, courteous and hospitable to strangers, respectful towards the old, kindly to children, helpful and loyal to his neighbours, the very embodiment of the virtues enjoined by the Incas—'do not steal, do not lie, do not be slothful'. Each of these contradictory views may hold some truth. So long as he lives within his own community and environment, the Indian adheres to the moral code traditional to his race. Uproot him and drive him into the white man's world, and he will appear inept and degenerate. He becomes like the respectable citizen whose country has come under enemy occupation and so makes a virtue of committing crimes he would never dream of in normal times; to cheat and steal, skimp his work, and even stab his master in the back if given the chance. The Indian's homeland has been under enemy occupation for more than four centuries, so that this double standard has become his second nature.

It is this attitude which makes the Indian so resistant to the call of 'progress'. Preservation of what remains of his old way of life rather than progress towards the goals of the white man has been his traditional concern. He is not easily convinced that the new techniques he is being exhorted to adopt are not some fresh form of covert exploitation. The agrarian adviser, the social worker, and the educational reformer thus often find themselves up against a wall of suspicion and incomprehension. Nor, it seems, can it be left to the pull of economic interest to bring the Indian into the modern world. For the most part, he still lives outside, or on the fringe of, the money economy. If he earns, it is so that he may subsist; if he sets anything at all aside, it is for the fiesta where he will lavish it on food, drink, and entertainment to win prestige in the eyes of his fellows.

Membership of an Indian community does not encourage the emergence of wealthy individuals but the maintenance of a uniform degree of poverty through the dissipation of whatever surplus may be temporarily acquired. The virtues of self-improvement and saving which have shaped our capitalist society are not the virtues of the Indian.

Nevertheless, some change there has been in recent years. Since the large estates were broken up by the revolutionary land reform of 1953, the Indians of Bolivia have begun to emerge from the hopeless servitude depicted in *Raza de Bronce*. In Ecuador the *huasipungos* of Icaza's novel have now been at least legally abolished. In Peru the Indians' demands to own their own land are being pressed with renewed vigour. A fresh impulse has been given to the study and use of Quechua, and it is even claimed that we may witness a 'Quechuan Renaissance', the consequences of which might be an awakening of an Indian political nationalism, just as the Slav literary renaissance of the last century gave rise to the establishment of the Slav nation-states of central and south-east Europe.

If the Indian appears to be struggling free from the cruder forms of material exploitation he remains exposed to a more subtle exploitation at the hands of the non-Indian. Politicians are beginning to discover that a demagogic appeal to the Quechua- and Aymara-speaking population of the Andes may yield good dividends. The Communists of Guatemala have tried to gain a hearing amongst their Indians by retelling the ancient myths and equating the maleficent Lords of Xibalba with the Yanqui Imperialists. The Indians are only likely to know real emancipation when the non-Indian no longer tries to force or entice him into his own world and for his own purposes, and seeks instead to reshape his own institutions in such a way that the Indians may feel that they can take their place within them without doing violence to their traditional values. The Indian problem, in short, is to a large extent the problem of the white man's attitude towards the Indian. So far in this study we have been chiefly aware of the negative aspects of this attitude; the incomprehension, injustice, and callousness with which the white man has too often treated him. It is now time to turn to the positive achievements which resulted from the white man's coming and fashioned the culture of Spain's colonial empire and the mind of modern Latin America.

2
The Spanish Imprint

> 'The Spaniards gave beasts of burden to relieve the natives of drudgery, wool to wear for modesty's sake, for choice as well as necessity, and meat to eat which they lacked before. The Spaniards showed them the use of iron and of oil lamps to improve their ways of living; they gave them a system of money so that they would know how to buy and sell and what they had and owed. They taught them Latin and other subjects which are worth a lot more than all the silver taken from them, because with literacy they become men, whereas the silver was of little or no advantage to them. And so it was to their benefit to be conquered, and even more, to become Christians.'
>
> LÓPEZ DE GÓMARA

> 'Wherever else in the world have rational men in happy and populous lands been subjugated by such cruel and unjust wars called Conquests, and then been divided up by the same cruel butchers and tyrannical robbers as though they were inanimate things, have been enslaved in an infernal way, worse than in Pharaoh's day, treated like cattle being weighed in the meat market and—God save the mark—are looked upon as of less worth than bedbugs? How can the word of those who support such iniquities be believed?'
>
> BARTOLOMÉ DE LAS CASAS

The year in which America was discovered also saw the fall of Granada, the last Moslem kingdom remaining in Spain. Columbus himself witnessed the scene. 'I watched the Moorish king come out to the city gates and kiss your royal hands', he later reminded his sovereigns. The two great enterprises of *Reconquista* and *Conquista* were indeed intimately related. The New World was won by men whose beliefs and outlook had been forged in the epic achievement of Spain's Middle Age. The mentality of the first European settlers was thus compounded of medieval no less than renaissance traits which left their impress on the life of the colonial period.

Character of the 'conquistadores'

The *conquistadores* were a breed of men never surpassed for courage, endurance, and unquenchable energy. 'When, either in ancient or in modern times, have such great exploits been wrought by so few against so many, under so many climes, across such distant seas and lands, for the conquest of the unseen and the unknown?' boasted Francisco Xérez, who had served as secretary to Pizarro in Peru. 'And those who took part in the various campaigns were neither paid nor pressed, but went of their own free will and at their own expense. And thus, in our own days, they have conquered more territory than that which all the princes, either Christian or infidel, were hitherto known to possess, subsisting on the savage food of men who knew neither bread nor wine, making do with herbs and roots and fruits for food; and yet they have conquered what all the world knows.'

The *conquistadores* were men of differing social background. Many were of the humblest origins—the illegitimate, the dispossessed, the vagrants. Not a few were *hidalgos*—youths of good family but poor prospects. After the spectacular fortunes made in Mexico and Peru scions of the highest nobility became eager to join in. But those most needed for orderly settlement, the labourers and peasant farmers, were in short supply. Even when the Crown sought to encourage their migration all sorts of obstacles were placed in their way by Spanish landowners loath to see their estates denuded of labour. Of those who did succeed in volunteering as colonists, many later exchanged the plough for the sword and threw in their lot with the soldiers of fortune. The latter were recruited from all parts of Spain. The desolate frontier region of Estremadura supplied a specially large quota. Strong contingents came from Portugal, and some from Italy. The Emperor's German subjects also claimed a share in the *Conquista*, particularly in Venezuela where they outdid the Spaniards in destructive fury, if not in colonising achievements. Even Englishmen occasionally found their way into the expeditions, and there is a record of a couple serving in de Soto's ill-fated campaign in Florida who are mentioned for their ability to outshoot the warlike natives with their English long-bows.

The motives which animated the *conquistadores* were the urge to make a fortune, to win fame, power, and rank, and to satisfy their love of adventure. In pursuing these objectives, the *conquistadores* were also convinced that they were at the same time serving God and their King. 'We came here to serve God and also to get rich,' declared Bernal Díaz, a soldier of Cortés. Though he might more properly have inverted the order of the sentence, there is no cause to doubt his sincerity. The Spanish medieval mind saw no contradiction in serving God and getting rich. Had not Spain's national hero, the Cid, done great service to God and the King by winning fresh lands from the Moors, and grown enormously rich, famous, and powerful in the process? Gold itself was invested with an almost mystical quality. 'Gold is most excellent', wrote Columbus, who dreamed one day of using his new wealth to finance a crusade to the

Holy Land. 'Of gold is treasure made; with gold, the possessor of it does all that he desires in the world and may even send souls to paradise.' The direct acquisition of gold was esteemed a far nobler aim than the creation of wealth through agriculture or commerce. When offered an estate on Hispaniola, the youthful Cortés replied: 'I came to get gold, not to till the soil like a peasant.' And the sardonic side of the Spanish genius finds expression in his ironic message to the Mexican notables explaining that the Spaniards were men suffering from a disease of the heart which could only be relieved by gold.

The *conquistadores* were adventurers, but adventurers under royal licence. The latter was known as a 'Capitulation'—a term which carries misleading associations, since it has no connotation of 'surrender', but takes its name from the several clauses, or chapters, which composed the agreement. These defined the *conquistador*'s rights of exploration, trade, conquest, and colonisation, and the specific and general obligations which he in turn assumed (including penalties for their non-observance), and the favours, privileges, and financial rewards which he might claim if his enterprise prospered. The *conquistador*, for his part, undertook to cover the expenses of the expedition (though the Crown might contribute a share), raise the armed force, and, if required, enlist settlers. He was also pledged to set aside the fifth part of all booty for the King, to found the requisite number of forts and settlements, to treat the natives well and to see to their conversion. The Capitulations thus provided a legal framework within which the individual could pursue his personal ambitions. The officers of the Crown, it is true, were often hard put to it to enforce compliance with the terms agreed upon, and some of the most spectacular exploits, such as the conquest of Mexico by Cortés, were accomplished without prior mandate, but the *conquistador*'s loyalty to the Crown was never in question. They might cut off the head of a viceroy sent out to enforce the unpopular new laws of the Indies, but they would do so in the name of the King. History records only one of their number, the tyrant Aguirre, who openly repudiated the royal authority and attempted to set up on his own.

The *Conquista* was a product of three interrelated and often concurrent processes: discovery and exploration, military conquest, settlement and colonisation. The pioneers were chiefly discoverers and explorers. Others explored and clashed with the natives but made no settlements. The greatest—or most fortunate—of the *conquistadores* first discovered, then conquered, and finally settled their territories. Some Spaniards, especially the latecomers, were too turbulent to do more than handle the sword. But the authentic *conquistador* was by instinct far more than a mere soldier and cherished the colonist's passion to possess the land he discovered. Bernal Díaz relates how, soon after landing on the mainland, before Mexico had been conquered or even explored, he had planted a fistful of orange pips which he had brought with him, and how, years later, he returned to that spot and had the grown trees transplanted to the estate which he had meanwhile won for himself. In a letter to the King, Pedro de Valdivia, the conqueror of Chile, summed up the role of the *conquistador* towards his men:

'A Captain to encourage them in war, and to be the first in danger, as was fitting; a father, to help them as I could and to grieve for their toils, aiding them like sons to endure; and a friend to speak with them; a land-surveyor to trace out and colonise; an overseer to make channels and to share out water;

a tiller and worker at the sowings; a head-shepherd for the breeding of flocks, and, in short, settler, breeder, defender, conqueror, and discoverer.'

Chronicles, poems, and histories

Valdivia might have added to his list: chronicler and man of letters. The same irrepressible urge which sent the Spaniards across uncharted seas and towering mountains drove them at times to take up the pen instead of the sword. The desire to record and understand the marvels of the New World, and to win fame for the part they had played in its conquest, was in itself a challenge to heroic action. 'My only rest was to weary myself with writing', declared Pedro Cieza de León, author of a vast chronicle of the conquest of Peru. 'But neither the roughness of the land, nor the mountains, nor rivers, nor yet intolerable hunger and privation could weaken my twin purpose of writing and of following my Captain and my flag.' Alonso de Ercilla y Zúñiga, the celebrated soldier poet, tells us that much of his epic *La Araucana* was written in the thick of a campaign against the formidable warriors of Chile, and was 'often penned on hides for lack of paper, and on scraps of letters so small that there was scarce room enough for six verses together'. Even the most illiterate soldier would be familiar with the traditional *romances* or ballads of Spain, and would turn to them, or to the books of knight errantry, then much in vogue, for parallels to the fantastic adventures which they themselves were experiencing. When his companions first beheld Montezuma's fabulous capital of Tenochtitlán, Bernal Díaz writes that 'we were all struck with amazement and exclaimed that the towers, temples, and lakes seemed like the enchantments we read of in *Amadis*'. From another romance of chivalry, Cortés himself took the name California—'an island very close to the terrestrial paradise'—for one of his later discoveries. Sometimes a moving experience would itself inspire the composition of a ballad such as the *romance* describing Cortés gazing in grief towards an Aztec temple where two of his companions, captured in battle a short while before, are being dragged off for sacrifice.

The production of reports, letters, narratives, and chronicles was also encouraged by the Crown as a means of detecting abuses of power or mistakes of policy as well as furnishing general information. The *conquistador* needed to report fully and promptly to the Crown in order to secure the confirmation of the privileges promised him in his Capitulations. He might also feel impelled, in order to attract settlers to the newly discovered land or for some other reason, to arouse the admiration and approval of the public. Columbus appears to have had this in mind in composing the famous letter announcing his momentous discovery. Studiously vague in its navigational information, its lyrical evocation of a strange and exuberantly lovely island inhabited by innocent savages waiting to receive the true faith and to reveal the secrets of their goldmines was well calculated to excite the curiosity, the covetousness, and the idealism of mankind. Where the *conquistador* had acted without a specific mandate it was still more vital for him to report matters in such a way as to placate the Crown, forestall or outmanœuvre rivals, and to justify questionable actions. The *cartas-relaciones* of Hernán Cortés are masterpieces of this nature. It was, incidentally, their tendency to play down the achievements of the great captain's comrades-in-arms—a tendency later intensified in the history of the conquest written by his chaplain Gómara—which stirred one of his old soldiers to take up his pen in retirement and give posterity his own inimitable version of the extraordinary story.

Bernal Díaz del Castillo's *History of the Conquest of New Spain* gives an unforgettable panorama of the conquest, enlivened by vivid portraits of his captains and comrades-in-arms and of Montezuma and other Aztec chiefs. To read his pages is to have the sensation of actually overhearing the gossip round the camp-fires, of listening to the banter, the grousing, the forebodings, and the boasting of the *conquistadores.* We shudder with them at the booming of the Aztec war-drums. We learn the names and qualities of each of their war-horses. No detail is too trivial for him—or for us; Bernal Díaz (? 1492–1581) is a master, for all his avowed artlessness, in weaving them together as his narrative mounts to its climax. He tells his tale with a down-to-earth directness which commands confidence. Not for him the embellishments of Gómara and some later historians, who claim that St James himself miraculously appeared on the field of battle to lead the Christians to victory. 'It may be as Gómara says,' comments Bernal Díaz, 'but if so, all I can say is that I, poor sinner, was not worthy to see it. What I know I did see was Francisco de Morla who came riding up on his chestnut horse with Cortés. Now, as I write these lines, I seem to see him with these sinner's eyes of mine, and the whole course of the war and how we fared in it. . . .'

One early copy of Gómara's history has been preserved which contains two sets of annotations written by different hands in the margin. One set clearly stems from a veteran of the conquest of Peru who, like Bernal Díaz in Mexico, is often stirred to resentment by Gómara's account. 'Lies!', 'Idiot!', 'Knave!' the anonymous *conquistador* frequently exclaims.

The second commentator is more restrained and urbane in his comments, promising that 'God grant us His grace and some years of life, and we shall correct many of the errors which this History contains, notably those relating to the customs of the natives of this country and their land'. The pledge was kept, and in due course the Inca Garcilaso de la Vega's *Comentarios Reales*, which we have referred to in the preceding chapter, was given to the world.

Nor did the *conquistadores* record only their triumphs. One of the most remarkable of their narratives is that left by Alvar Núñez Cabeza de Vaca (?1490–?1559), who served in an ill-fated expedition to Florida. Here we see the *Conquista* in reverse; for the Spanish survivors became not the masters but the slaves of the Indians they had set out to subdue. But their leader, by force of personality and astonishing fortitude, gradually asserted his ascendency over his captors, and then trekked from one side of the continent to the other healing the sick and quelling the tribal rivalries of the Indians until he was at last reunited with his own people. Another strange tale of captivity is the *Cautiverio Feliz* of Núñez de Pineda y Bascuñán (1607–1682), who fell into the hands of the warlike Araucanians in the following century. Stripped of its passages of tedious moralising, the book relates the adventures of a young Spaniard alternately hounded by bloodthirsty chiefs and sheltered by friendly Indians, whose life of idyllic simplicity and virtue he describes with great charm.

The Araucanian frontier is also the setting for a still more famous work, the first indeed to treat of America with conscious literary intent: *La Araucana* (1569–89) by Alonso de Ercilla y Zúñiga (? 1533–1594). The theme of this epic is the interminable warfare, in which he himself played a part, waged against the Indians by the Spaniards on the southernmost bounds of their empire; warfare which continued throughout the whole colonial period until far into the nineteenth century, with profound effects on the social and psychological evolution of the Chilean nation. In Ercilla's majestic lines the Indian chiefs, Lautaro, Galvarino, Caupolicán, achieve heroic stature; and since a recital of even the most stupendous feats of arms may end by wearying the reader, the poet is constantly breaking off his narrative to relate some romantic tale of love or some touch of the supernatural. *La Araucana* is accounted by many to be the best epic in the Spanish language, and if its Spanish author can be considered Latin American through choice of theme and treatment, its composition lays the foundation for a Latin American literature.

Whilst the men of action were writing their memoirs, or transmuting their visions of events into epic verse, the historians were busy trying to construct a broader framework for this mass of first-hand material. The first official historiographer of the Indies, working in the convenient staging-post of Hispaniola, was Fernández de Oviedo y Valdés (1478–1557). His work is far more than a catalogue of military exploits, for his curiosity ranges over the whole field of new experience opened up by the discovery of the New World, and he has left us a compendium of those aspects of its natural history which a European observer would find most fascinating for their novelty, together with descriptions of the customs and ways of life of the Indian tribes of which he had knowledge. Though censuring the cruelty of individual *conquistadores*, Oviedo shares his compatriots' general pride in Spain's achievement. Far different was the view of Bartolomé de las Casas (1474–1565), the ex-*conquistador* turned friar, who denounced the *Conquista* as an unmitigated evil. 'It is through the arrogance of Hernán Cortés and the historians who have chronicled his deeds in the Spanish tongue that the whole world has been cunningly deceived', he wrote. 'For he and they have but one and the same aim, namely to make themselves rich at the cost of the blood of those wretched, humble, and peace-loving peoples, like men heedless of the evils they praise and condone. Everything they write is but framed to excuse the tyrannies and abominable acts of Cortés and the others, and to disparage and condemn the poor, defenceless Indians.' It was with the passionate desire to prove this thesis and arouse the conscience of the nation that Las Casas composed his voluminous *Historia de las Indias* and the famous *Brevísima Relación de la Destrucción de las Indias.*

The great debate

This brings us to a consideration of the *Conquista* in terms of the 'Black Legend' which has coloured the thinking of Spain's traditional rivals for the spoils of the New World. The brutality of many of the *conquistadores,* their cruel subjugation and merciless exploitation of the natives, cannot be denied. The scale of their achievement was grandiose, and their crimes were often in proportion. What is less generally realised is the indignant repudiation of those crimes by their more humane compatriots, and the sustained endeavours of the Crown to apply remedies and safeguards. Matters indeed went much further; denunciation of crimes broadened into a prolonged and nation-wide debate, in which the humblest friar could make his voice heard no less than the parvenu landowner, regarding the ethics of the *Conquista* itself, the nature of the Indians, and the rights of Spain to wage war and exercise sovereignty. 'It does honour to the sixteenth-century Spanish mind', writes a Latin American scholar, 'that the controversy could arise even against "reason of state", and it is interesting to compare the mental outlook of a Bartolomé de las Casas, who was still living on the borderland between the Middle Ages and the Renaissance, with that of a modern poet such as Kipling, the bard of British imperialism in India.'

The opening round was the public denunciation by Dominican friars in Hispaniola, less than twenty years after Columbus had landed there, of the *conquistadores*' maltreatment of the natives: 'Are not these Indians men? Do not they have rational souls? Are you not obliged to love them as you love yourselves?' How, indeed, could a Christian prince be justified in waging war against a part of mankind which, deprived of the light of the Gospel, had given him no cause for offence? The Crown's first attempt to grapple with the problem was to order that its Captains, before undertaking any military operations against the natives, should first give them a chance of submitting peacefully after explaining to them the rudiments of the Christian faith and the authority vested in the King of Spain by the Pope, God's representative on earth, to take them under his protection for the good of their souls. This was all set out in a lengthy document known as the *Requerimiento* or Summons which had to be read out to the natives through an interpreter. If, after this had been done, the natives still refused to submit, they could be considered as 'rebels', and the Spaniards were authorised to use force against them. It was scarcely to be expected that the Spanish adventurers would take the *Requerimiento* seriously, or that, if they did, the Indians would be able to make head or tail of it. Bartolomé de las Casas tells us that he did not himself know whether to laugh or weep at it.

The man who was later to earn the title of Defender of the Indians began life as a *conquistador*, and even after his conversion he retained much of the vehemence, impulsiveness, and unquenchable energy of the men whose misdeeds he denounced. Las Casas believed passionately that only persuasion and pacific means should be used to christianise the Indians. His own attempts to establish a settlement on this basis ended in complete failure. Thereafter he devoted his life to stirring the conscience of his countrymen, including the King and his counsellors, in favour of the Indians. His influence may be found in the vast body of painstaking legislation known as the New Laws of the Indies (1542). A heavy-handed attempt to introduce these laws into Peru provoked rebellion and the slaying of the Viceroy. Opposition, both on the part of the vested interests of *conquistadores* and of conservative thinkers in Spain, enflamed the controversy still more bitterly. The King felt his royal conscience so troubled in the matter that he actually proclaimed a halt to any further expeditions whilst a conclave of learned jurists, theologians, and officials was summoned to consider 'how conquests, discoveries, and settlements can be made to accord with justice and reason'. Here Las Casas faced Ginés de Sepúlveda, the eminent jurist and commentator of Aristotle, who claimed that the Indians belonged to the category of 'natural slaves', destined by their congenital savagery and incapacity to be subdued by arms and reduced to servitude by the Christians as an essential preliminary to their christianisation. Las Casas stoutly held that 'the savage peoples of the earth may be compared to uncultivated soil that readily brings forth weeds and useless thorns, but has within itself such natural virtues that by labour and cultivation it may be made to yield sound and beneficial fruits'.

The outcome of the duel between Las Casas and Sepúlveda was inconclusive, each contestant claiming that the victory had been his. The conflict indeed was never resolved, for it reflects opposing attitudes of mind which, as we have seen in the previous chapter, have led writers and politicians to take widely differing views of the worth of the Indian. The humanism of Las Casas, for all his exaggerations and errors of judgment (he advocated the introduction of negro slaves as a means of alleviating the Indians' distress), seems to accord most nearly with our way of thinking today. To the Latin Americans the great debate is of more than historical importance. As a contemporary thinker has put it: 'On the borderland where the violence of the *conquistador* and the ethical humanism of the Laws of the Indies meet, and where Las Casas battled the Spanish overlords, we come nearer—above and beyond all propaganda—to the reality of our beginnings.'

'*Conquistador*' *into colonist*

The *conquistador*, as we have noted, was also a settler. He had to decide when and where to take formal possession of the newly discovered land and to found the first settlement. The latter would at first be little more than a collection of rough wooden cabins laid out on the standard chessboard pattern, with an empty square in the centre flanked by the church and the public buildings, including the prison, the storehouse, and the governor's residence. But this makeshift accommodation would be replaced as soon as possible by substantial and often impressive stone structures which sometimes gave a dignity, size, and spaciousness to the new cities surpassing the older foundations of the mother-country. So wisely did the Spaniards choose their sites, and so rapidly did the vast territory become studded with their settlements, that today there is scarcely a city of any magnitude in Spanish America which was not founded before 1600. City-building had a calculated and important place in the whole process of the *Conquista*. The Laws of the Indies laid down that 'every city in Spanish America should evoke wonder in the Indians when they saw it, so that they would thereby understand that the Spaniards were permanently settled there and, accordingly, should be feared and respected, their friendship sought, and no offence given'.

The establishment of cities also answered other needs. The *conquistadores* were hungry for rank and status, and the honourable offices of *alcalde*, *regidor*, and the like flattered these aspirations, as well as bringing with them valuable economic privileges and perquisites. Municipal offices provided a constructive outlet for their energies once military duties no longer claimed them. They also constituted a fount of legal authority which astute leaders such as Cortés understood how to turn to good account. Lacking a proper mandate from the Crown and aware that the Governor in whose name he had been sent wanted to take over the Conquest for himself, Cortés lost no time in founding his first settlement at Vera Cruz and getting the newly elected municipal officers to nominate him as their provisional Governor. But though vigorous initiative stemming from the cities might promote the *Conquista* in its early stages, the Crown was wary, especially after the revolt of the *Comuneros* in Spain during the 1520s, and soon placed curbs on the independence of the new municipalities. Office-holders were appointed rather than elected, and placed under the control of full-time officials sent out from Spain. Though they retained their wealth and social position, the early colonists and their descendants found their administrative and political power curtailed. This gave rise to frustrations and resentment against the placemen from Spain which were amongst the roots of the later movement for independence.

The cities gave an urban character to Spain's colonial civilisation. But they produced no class of merchant-princes as, for instance, in renaissance Italy, for trade was still looked down upon, and power and wealth remained based on the great estates. New settlers from Spain, and even the officials sent by the Crown to hold the power of the creoles in check, bought or married their way into the landed aristocracy. The latter, whether exercising untrammelled sway on their *haciendas* or residing in the cities, were divided from the Indian and *mestizo* masses by vast disparities of culture no less than by their social status. Universities had been founded in the new cities and began to train a long line of lawyers, theologians, and humanists. They were open only to the sons of the 'oligarchy', and attuned not to the requirements of their American environment, but to the traditional European pattern. Even the work of a *mestizo* so conscious of his Indian heritage as the Inca Garcilaso de la Vega was, as we have seen, cast in the mould of Spanish culture. Ruiz de Alarcón, possibly the most brilliant literary figure to be born and bred in the Indies, won fame on the Spanish stage. Though patriotic critics claim to detect subtle Mexican influences in his work, the latter is generally accounted to belong wholly to the literature of Spain and so falls outside the scope of this book.

As *conquistador* gave place to colonist, so conservative-minded clerics followed in the wake of adventurous friars. Though a few priests had been little more than *conquistadores* in cassocks, who believed in beating the new faith into the natives, many had shown remarkable devotion and imagination in rendering it intelligible to the aboriginal mind. They made profound studies of the Indians' languages and customs. Sahagún's monumental work, compiled with the co-operation of the natives, remains an essential source for our knowledge of Mexican antiquity and the corner-stone of ethnological studies. Others, like Pedro de Gante, devoted themselves to integrating the Indians into the new society as artisans and craftsmen. Vasco de Quiroga went still further; influenced by his study of Moore's *Utopia*, he built up in his diocese of Michoacán a remarkable complex of interrelated native communities, each specialising in the production of its own wares—lacquer-work, footwear, wood-carving, etc.—and equipped with communal hospital, granaries, and other services. But this great impetus for evangelisation, study, and social transformation, though it was still to produce remarkable fruit in certain areas of the New World, as in the Jesuit settlements of Paraguay, was soon spent. The Church acquired land, grew rich, and religion was formalised into religiosity. The stultifying hand of the Inquisition was stretched over the land. Indians, as infants in the faith, were mercifully outside its jurisdiction, and it could find few Judaisers or heretics to deal with except for the occasional Protestant prisoner who was unlucky enough to fall into Spanish hands. So the Inquisitors busied themselves particularly with such matters as the suppression of sorcery, the supervision of books, and the enforcement of the correct norms of ecclesiastical jurisdiction and precedence. The age of heroic action was over; the Counter-Reformation permitted no adventuring in the dangerous field of ideas. Creole energies could find outlet only in the refinements and varieties of external form. The stage was set for the flowering of the baroque.

The age of the baroque

Latin America's Baroque Age seems to us curiously remote and alien today; more so, in many respects, than the *Conquista* with its trauma always discernible beneath the surface of modern life, or the ancient pre-Columbian civilisations whose monuments and works of art readily excite our admiration and invite our study. But the baroque has left its mark more deeply than we may realise. 'In spite of nearly two centuries of rationalism and modern criticism', a leading authority assures us, 'we Spanish Americans have not yet emerged fully from its labyrinth. It still heavily influences our aesthetic sensibility and the many complex aspects of our collective psychology.' We see the force of this remark if we turn to the work of such contemporary writers as the gifted Cuban novelist Alejo Carpentier (1904–). His *Pasos Perdidos* (1955), which tells the story of a European-educated Latin American intellectual who returns to the tropical forest where he becomes aware of the cultural origins of his race, is a richly wrought work cast in an essentially baroque mould.

Architecture is the art which most splendidly expresses and preserves the spirit of the baroque. Its impact is all the stronger for the popular elements which have clearly fused with it. Ornately magnificent churches, which convey the majesty of the state religion, take the place of the austere single-naved structures built by the missionary friars. But though their design is Spanish, we discern a native hand in their construction. Indian motifs have been introduced into the ornamentation, and local deities reappear under the image of Christian saints. We note the same trends in painting and sculpture; in the grace of the coloured carvings of Ecuador and in the paintings of Cuzco, where the Virgin Mary wears the puffed skirts and broadbrimmed hat of the *chola* or *mestiza.* In the minor arts, particularly in ceramics, embroidery, silver-ware, and basketry, we find the baroque humanised by popular artistry.

It is in the field of letters that the baroque now appears least accessible to us. Which authors of the period can we name, which works of theirs do we still read? The true flavour of the period is perhaps conveyed less by its own literary production than by the brilliant reconstruction of colonial life evoked in the ten volumes of Ricardo Palma's (1833–1919) *Tradiciones Peruanas* (1872–1906). The *Tradiciones* treat of viceregal escapades and episcopal intrigues, of the piety, self-seeking, and lavish ceremonial of the City of Kings and its picaresque fringe. Etched with irony and picturesque verve, these vignettes of history, legend, fantasy, and sociological marginalia strike a completely new note in Latin American letters.

The society evoked with such brilliance in Palma's pages was not marked by provincial philistinism or literary stagnation. Letters were a serious concern, in some quarters even an obsession. But this concern arose generally from causes which have little interest for us and expressed itself in forms which strike us as artificial, perhaps scarcely comprehensible. It was a literature both ephemeral and esoteric: esoteric, since it was written by and for an élite, trained in the classics and much given to the current cult of elaborate metaphors and conceits, recondite allusions, and stylistic virtuosity; ephemeral, since it was generally produced to celebrate an occasion such as the arrival of a viceroy, the birth of a prince, or the anniversary of a city's foundation. A feature of these celebrations was the literary contest, in which scores of aspiring poets might present their odes, sonnets, or rhymed conceits. For the less literary-minded, and of course for the Indian and *mestizo* masses, there were the processions and the sumptuous ritual of the church services, the bull-fights and tournaments, the *autos sacramentales* and the masquerades, which were such a striking manifestation of the baroque culture of the great cities. An account of one of these processions in Lima significantly records that the figure of Luís de Góngora, the foremost exponent of Spain's new literary fashion, was accorded a place of honour beside those of Homer and Virgil. An apologia for Góngora, written by the erudite *mestizo* Juan de Espinosa Medrano (1632–1688), also ranks as one of the most interesting work of literary criticism to be produced during the colonial period.

The voices which speak to us most clearly today from this vanished world of the baroque are those of two writers who, in their very different ways, lived only on its fringes—a disreputable shopkeeper of Lima and a celebrated Mexican nun. For Juan del Valle Caviedes (?1652–?1697) there was no place in the university or the viceregal court. What money he once possessed was squandered on women and gambling, and his shattered health brought him into the clutches of doctors whose pretentious malpractices he never ceased from pillorying in his corrosive satire. Nothing escaped his sharp eye and his savage tongue; not even the miserable prostitute whose death in a Lima hospital inspired his 'To the fair Arnada', surely one of the cruellest pieces of raillery in the Spanish language. Caviedes has been compared with Molière, and, more aptly, with Quevedo. Though lacking his mannered sophistication, the author of the well-named *Diente de Parnaso* yields nothing in mordant ferocity to the Spanish moralist. There is a direct, hard-hitting quality about Caviedes which sets him apart from his contemporaries; but his obsession with death and corruption, and the pessimism of his view of life as a dream in which evil masquerades as good, are characteristic of the baroque spirit.

If Caviedes prided himself on being a man who had learned more from looking into human nature than into books, Sor Juana Inés de la Cruz (? 1651–1695) was a being for whom learning was a passion and poetry as natural a form of expression as gossip is to most women. In delightful pages of autobiography she has described how, as a child, she cut off her hair and would not let it grow again until she had mastered some difficulty in her self-imposed studies, since 'it was not fitting that a head so bereft of reason should be so bedeckt with tresses'. By the age of sixteen she had achieved such a command of the classics, philosophy, law, mathematics, and other subjects that the Viceroy himself summoned a panel of scholars to test the learning of this prodigy. She emerged with flying colours, 'like a royal galleon beating off the attacks of a few sloops', the Viceroy commented. Nor was this Mexican girl a desiccated bluestocking; she was blessed with charm, beauty, and sweet temper. But she had no fortune. For this reason, or perhaps—if we are to attribute an autobiographical inspiration to her love-poetry—because she may have suffered some bitter affair of the heart, she decided to leave the splendours of the court for the security of a convent. The Hieronymite Order, which she entered, was the most liberal of seventeenth-century Mexico, and her ample cell, crammed with books and with musical and scientific instruments, soon became a centre of the country's intellectual and literary life.

Sonnets, allegories, plays sacred and profane, occasional verse of every description, some in Latin as well as Spanish, all couched in witty and highly rhetorical vein, continued to pour from the convent. How much of it survives as literature today?

Some of the shorter pieces, notably the famous verses *Against the Inconsequence of Men*, have a well-earned place in anthologies. Though Sor Juana's poetry generally speaks to the head rather than the heart, the best of her *autos sacramentales*, *El Divino Narciso*, achieves a mystic intensity of feeling in its allegory of Christ's love for the divine image reflected in human nature redeemed by Grace. Perhaps her most interesting composition, as well as the most difficult on account of its baroque richness and intricacy, is the long poem called *Primer Sueño*, in which the mind, freed by sleep, soars up in its craving to encompass the totality of knowledge but falls back frustrated as dawn announces a return to the workaday world. Was not this Sor Juana's own tragedy? Though the convent offered security and a certain tolerance for literary activity, the very range and power of her genius aroused misgivings. When forbidden the use of books, her mind drew on the commonest objects for her restless observation and speculation. She would muse on the spiral movement of a child's spinning top and deduce principles from the frying of an egg ('If Aristotle had done some cooking, he would have found still more to write about', she observed). One day she was asked by her mother superior to compose a refutation of a sermon by the famous preacher Antonio de Vieira.[1] She did so in terms which connoisseurs in theological disputation agree to have demolished the thesis of the Jesuit. But the completeness of Sor Juana's triumph proved her undoing. She was reproved by a bishop, writing under the pseudonym of Sor Filotea, for having wasted her talents in literary frivolities. The nun replied in her moving and brilliant apologia, *Respuesta a Sor Filotea* (1691). Then she fell silent, sold her cherished books and instruments, and

1. See p. 125

devoted the rest of her life to works of penitence and service to the community. The spiritual crisis which led to this renunciation can only be glimpsed. The exercise of the extraordinary talents 'given me, I know not whether for bane or blessing', as she had written, proved too dangerous for a woman living in an age when the cult of the baroque permitted all manner of ingenuity in formal invention, but when prudence imposed the most unquestioning orthodoxy of thought.

From enlightenment to independence

The baroque continued to flourish in Latin America for some time after the spirit of scientific enquiry known as the Enlightenment had established its sway over Europe. An almost medieval outlook still informs such works as Solórzano y Pereira's voluminous survey of colonial institutions, *Política Indiana* (1647), or the labours of the erudite Sigüenza y Góngora (1645–1700) to incorporate the Aztec deities into biblical and classical lore (e.g. Quetzalcoatl is identified with St Thomas and the Indians of the New World with the descendants of Poseidon, himself a great grandson of Noah). As late as 1784, students of physics in Argentina were still concerned with such problems as whether angels and demons could move objects corporeally. Learning was conceived as the accumulation of data on the basis established once and for all by sacrosanct authority; only the most daring minds ventured to scrutinise that basis itself. But in time the new outlook found adherents even in Spain; through the writings of such Spaniards as Feijoo, and through the policies of some of the eighteenth-century statesmen and administrators, the spirit of the Enlightenment began to permeate the climate of thought in the colonies.

The Enlightenment did not come to Spain as a gospel of

revolution. It was welcomed rather as a means of rescuing the country from its appalling backwardness through the promotion of 'useful knowledge'. For Spanish America it promised, and eventually produced, excellent results in revitalising such languishing fields as the once fabulous gold- and silver-mines. Societies pledged to educational, scientific, and civic progress were launched, and the first newspapers started—'very useful, provided they confine themselves to small matters', a Viceroy cautiously commented. Scientific enquiry and technical advance were also stimulated by a succession of expeditions undertaken by distinguished foreigners: Frezier (1713), La Condamine (1736), Bougainville (1767), Vancouver (1795), and above all by the monumental scientific and sociological investigations of the great Alexander von Humboldt (1769–1821). Spain also sent scientists of her own, some of them of the calibre of the naturalist Mutis (1732–1808), saluted by Linnaeus as 'immortal', and Jorge Juan and Antonio de Ulloa, authors of an interesting *Viaje a la América Meridional* (1748) and possibly also of the more sensational and famous *Noticias Secretas*. Nor were the scientists alone in describing the American scene. Satirical works, such as the entertaining *Lazarillo de ciegos caminantes* (? Lima, 1775), also made a furtive appearance. This curious work, a hotchpotch of anecdote, picaresque adventure, and sociological observation, is a traveller's handbook for the journey across the continent from Montevideo to Lima, allegedly written by Concolorcorvo, a *mestizo* who complains that his status precludes him from aspiring to any occupation more honourable than that of dog-catcher to the cathedral at Cuzco. In reality, the author was a Spaniard, Alonso Carrió de la Vandera (*circa* 1715–1779), who exercised the functions of an inspector of the postal services.

The spirit of scientific enquiry, irreverent questioning, and reformist zeal thus found adherents amongst Spaniards and Creoles alike. But whereas in Spain the Enlightenment was at first encouraged as a means of reinvigorating the administration and promoting the interests of the Crown, its effect in the colonies was inevitably to erode the royal authority. The Spanish advocates of the Enlightenment wanted reforms which would promote a more progressive and efficient, but also a more centralised, despotism; the Creoles wanted reforms offering them more scope for running their own affairs and freer markets for their growing trade. Many of them came into direct touch with the ideas of the Enlightenment through their travels in Europe, and through such works by foreign, particularly French, writers as were introduced into America. The book trade was flourishing, and less hampered by the Inquisition, at least up to the time of the French Revolution, than might have been expected; banned books could, in any case, often be obtained through contraband channels. Latin America thus became acquainted with the work not only of thinkers like Newton and Descartes, but of more disturbingly political writers such as Voltaire, Montesquieu, Rousseau, and Raynal, whose *Histoire des Indes* had acquired such popularity outside Spain that it went through more than fifty editions by the end of the century. This impassioned indictment of Spain's record in the New World was, in reality, a re-statement of the Black Legend, a further round in the Great Debate. But the disputants had now shifted their ground. Las Casas had denounced the actions of the secular arm as inconsistent with what he held to be sound Catholic doctrine; the philosophers of the Enlightenment attacked the Spanish Empire as permeated by clerical no less than by political obscurantism.

This image of an irremediably reactionary Spain continued to be propagated even when it was no longer true. Three years before the publication of Raynal's book, the Spanish Government had struck an important blow against clerical influence by expelling the Jesuits (1767) and thus, ironically, knocking away what had been one of the staunchest props of royal authority. To those who disliked its principles or envied its power, the Order appeared in the dangerous guise of a state within a state. It owned vast plantations throughout the New World, managed business and agricultural enterprises from the profits of which it financed its seminaries and missions, and governed great areas of Paraguay almost as an independent fief. In scholarship and letters the labours of the Jesuits had been no less impressive. At the end of the sixteenth century Father Acosta had written a celebrated work on America, weighing its realities against the hypotheses of Aristotle and other authorities and discreetly offering some original insights of his own (e.g. he was the first to postulate that the hemisphere may have been settled by tribes migrating overland from Asia). Two other Jesuits, Ovalle and Molina, composed notable and delightful studies of Chile which anticipate the work of the scientific investigators of the eighteenth century. No group of Europeans, in short, had identified themselves so fully with their adopted countries and studied them with such care, as had the Jesuits. It was not surprising that, after their expulsion, a note of nostalgia or resentment could be discerned in their writings. This is specially marked in the work of the expatriates from Mexico: Clavigero's *Ancient History of Mexico*, which extols the achievements of the Aztec past and the Indians' capacity for civilisation; Alegre's *Theological Institutions*, which looks back to Vasco de Quiroga's ventures in Christian utopia and forward to a new social order based equally on Catholic and democratic principles; Landívar's long poem extolling the land and people of Mexico, not for the benefits brought by the Spanish conquerors but for the virtues and simple life of its Indian inhabitants. Such works, being composed in exile and written in Italian or Latin, lie outside the scope of this book. But they are important in having contributed to arousing an interest in Latin America's past and in the promise of its future. Nor is it fortuitous that the *Letter to the South Americans*, the celebrated and widely disseminated tract demanding political independence for the colonists and accusing the mother country of unjustly depriving them of their liberties and properties, should come from the pen of a Jesuit writer, Vizcardo y Guzmán.

Before the close of the century, traditional values and modes of thought received the impact of two further shattering events; the French Revolution and the independence of the North American colonies. Few Creoles were radical enough to have welcomed the extension of the French upheaval to their own shores, but they eagerly continued to study the literature which had stimulated it and were quick to mark how sudden and complete the fall of the old order in Europe could be. The independence of the North American colonies offered an example which could be more unreservedly acclaimed, even if the Spanish colonies were still far from professing a similar goal for themselves. A mood of change was in the air. The Creoles were impatient for more freedom in running their own affairs and developing their trade. But only a handful of leaders worked deliberately for a complete break with Spain, and not even they were clear as to what form of government they wished to set up in its place. Should it be a European-style constitutional monarchy, a restored Incaic empire, or a republic? Such questions had scarcely begun to exercise their minds when the French armies crossed the Pyrenees, took the Spanish King prisoner, and presented the Creoles with their unprecedented opportunity. Colonies have been likened to fruit which must fall from the parent tree when ripe. But the Spanish colonies were torn from the branch by the storms sweeping over Europe. It is scarcely surprising that the fruit of their independence was to prove bitter to the taste.

3

A Mind in the Making

'We are independent, but we are not free; the arms of Spain no longer oppress us, but her traditions still weigh us down.'

ESTEBAN ECHEVERRÍA

'We shall never be great until the Spanish American feels himself to be just as Spanish as the sons of Spain.'

JOSÉ VASCONCELOS

'. . . whether perhaps the role of these lands in the history of man might not be to make possible for the first time certain symbioses of cultures.'

ALEJO CARPENTIER

Simón Bolívar, the greatest of those who fought for independence, had also the clearest intuition of the destiny which independence would bring. In his famous *Letter from Jamaica* (1815), composed during a pause in the fighting, he dismissed the expectation that the colonies, once free, should form a single mighty state as a Utopian dream. He went on to forecast with considerable prescience that the Creoles would form separate republics, possibly a monarchy in Mexico (where the establishment of an 'empire' was in fact attempted), that the Central Americans would form some federal grouping (which they did, though only for a short time), that what we now know as Colombia, Ecuador, and Venezuela should constitute one state though they might prefer to go their separate ways, that Buenos Aires would fall prey to military dictatorships, Peru suffer from the cleavage between the aristocracy and the underprivileged, and that Chile would enjoy good prospects for free and orderly development. Later, when it had become clear that the Creoles would indeed achieve their independence but that this would bring new problems in its train, he wrote to his friend Sucre: 'It may be said that I have liberated the New World, but it will not be said that I have achieved the stability and happiness of the nations which compose it.' Finally, after Sucre had been murdered, and Bolívar himself, like San Martín, O'Higgins, and the other great architects of independence, had gone into exile, he was led to write in bitter disillusionment: 'There is no good faith in America, nor amongst the nations of America. Treaties are scraps of paper; constitutions mere printed matter; elections, battles; and life a torment. . . . All who have laboured for the freedom of America have ploughed the sea.'

Bolívar was quicker than the other *próceres* of the independence to realise that, unless they corresponded to the realities of the Latin American environment and the capacity of the citizens, constitutions would remain 'mere printed matter'. The Creoles retained the legalistic cast of mind which had produced the Capitulations and the *Requerimiento* of the *Conquista* and the voluminous legislation of the colonial period. They ingenuously believed that the introduction of the perfect constitution would in itself produce a just, enlightened, and flourishing nation. If signs of this desirable transformation failed to appear, then clearly the constitution was at fault and needed to be changed. This belief has died hard, as witness the sixteen constitutions which Ecuador had in the course of one hundred and fifteen years. In reality, the search for magic legal formulae offered no escape from the dilemma which faced the young nations. They genuinely aspired to freedom; but political freedom, without a training in self-government and the discipline of a mature society, too readily degenerated—as Bolívar found—into anarchy. 'It is in vain that tyrants are destroyed by force of arms unless we establish a political order capable of making good the ravages of revolution', he wrote. But the only order of which the Latin Americans appeared capable was that of dictatorship. Thus the vicious circle, so long to plague the Latin American scene, was completed; freedom degenerating into anarchy, then dictators saving society from anarchy at the cost of their freedom. The dilemma, which Bolívar had perceived but could not save himself from, was well expressed by his old tutor, the great scholar Andrés Bello: 'No one loved liberty more sincerely than General Bolívar; but he, like everybody else, was caught up in the nature of things. Independence was necessary for Liberty, and the champion of Independence was, and had to be, a Dictator.'

Liberals and Conservatives

As far as popular liberties were concerned, independence thus seemed to have brought little change. Political power passed from the officials of the Crown to the Creole oligarchy, but the nature of society remained much as before. A lively and satirical picture of this society, as it was in Mexico on the eve of independence, is given in *El Periquillo Sarniento* (1816) by J. J. Fernández de Lizardi (1776–1827). This work, Latin America's first novel, is cast in the form of the picaresque adventure story in vogue in Spain a couple of centuries before. But the protagonist is less a rogue than a misfit, a victim of the corrupt practices and antiquated institutions satirised as he passes from school to prison, from apothecary's shop to notary's office. Beneath his comic verve, Lizardi writes with a didactic and reformist purpose. He attacks popular superstition and ignorance, the selfish and empty pretensions of those in power. Lizardi seems to have set little store by political independence as the cure for his country's ills. He chooses his targets not because they are Spanish, but because they seem to him to be abuses, which he believes may be set right with good will and the right use of reason. It is difficult to say whether his voice is that of the eighteenth-century Enlightenment, or that of the emerging Liberals of the nineteenth century.

We must, however, be on our guard against viewing Latin America in terms of our own constitutional and political development. The 'Liberal' and 'Conservative' parties which made their appearance in the new republics were not so much political parties as the *camarillas* of dictators. Those who thought of themselves as Liberals were generally receptive to progressive ideas from abroad and were often bitterly anti-clerical. Though well intentioned, they were sometimes led by their disregard of autochthonous realities into unfortunate results; such, we have seen, was the case when they abolished the colonial legislation designed to safeguard Indian status and property. The Conservatives, in their championship of Order, generally equated this with the closest possible approximation to the colonial *status quo*. Sometimes, as with Dr Francia in Paraguay, they proved successful in sealing off their countries from the contamination of new ideas and foreign contacts. At others, as with Porfirio Díaz in Mexico or Leguía in Peru, they welcomed foreign influence as a means of creating the new machinery of economic wealth and control which would perpetuate their regimes in power.

The classic example of the antagonism between Conservatives and Liberals is the prolonged duel fought out between

President García Moreno (1821–1875) and Juan Montalvo (1832–1889) of Ecuador. Though he had the dictator's customary energy and ruthlessness, which would not stop short at the execution or public flogging of his enemies, García Moreno was no ordinary tyrant. He was personally austere, incorruptible, a gifted writer, with a passionate interest in scientific matters. But first and foremost he was a religious fanatic, a throw-back to the Counter-Reformation, determined to drive his country physically into the modern era but spiritually back into the Middle Ages. On Good Fridays the President of the Republic would himself stagger through the streets of the capital under the weight of a great wooden cross, and see that his ministers joined in the penance. He concluded a concordat with the Vatican, recalled the Jesuits, supervised the reform of the clergy, reorganised the Army, conferring on his regiments such titles as Soldiers of the Infant Jesus, Volunteers of the Cross, and Guardians of the Virgin, and finally consecrated the whole country to the Sacred Heart of Jesus. Against this advance of the theocratic state, Montalvo raised the voice of impassioned Liberalism. First in Ecuador, and then from exile, he carried on an implacable duel with the dictator. And when the latter—'Regenerator of the Fatherland and martyr of Christian Civilisation' as his admirers called him—was struck down by assassination, the exile is alleged to have exclaimed: 'My pen has killed him!' The young Liberals who now embarked on their period of power assuredly drew inspiration from the master; but, as so frequently happens in Latin American history, 'revolution' proved of little benefit to the backward country. 'When I see what has befallen Ecuador after the death of García Moreno,' Montalvo wrote bitterly, as he turned his attack against a new brood of tyranny, 'I wish

I had let the Dictator live!' The Regenerator still has his partisans today, as has Montalvo, whose sequel to Don Quixote, *Capítulos que se le olvidaron a Cervantes*, and whose *Siete Tratados* (1882), rambling and ironic disquisitions in the manner of Montaigne, have won esteem as masterpieces of Spanish prose.

The old enmity between Conservatives and Liberals still persists in some parts of Latin America, though it has largely lost its original ideological basis. It has particularly afflicted Colombia, where the rival parties have reached a compromise by which Conservatives and Liberals peacefully alternate in power, and where, until very recently, bandit chiefs would demonstrate their loyalty to the party of their choice by exterminating the partisans of the other.

The need for 'mental emancipation'

In no part of Latin America did the aftermath of independence present a more deplorable picture of hopes dashed and tyranny triumphant than in the Argentine. After a brief period of enlightened dictatorship the young republic had succumbed to the bestial rule of Rosas. Men of humane and liberal views were forced into exile, many of them rallying round the Byronic figure of Esteban Echeverría (1805–1851) in Montevideo. Like so many of Latin America's leading writers, the Argentine poet devoted himself with equal ardour to politics and to letters. His poem *La Cautiva* (1837), a sentimental tale of love between two persons of differing race and destiny, set the vogue for romanticism in the nascent literature of Latin America. The new nations, he held, needed to create art and letters of their own. They needed, above all, to develop a new mentality untrammelled by the old colonial attitudes. 'The body has won freedom, but not the mind', he wrote in his *Dogma Socialista*

(1838). 'We are independent, but we are not free; the arms of Spain no longer oppress us, but her traditions still weigh us down.' The political revolution which the liberators had made must be followed by a social revolution, and 'the social emancipation of America can only be achieved by repudiating the heritage bequeathed by Spain'. In its place he called for an order based on the synthesis of individual rights and social obligations. What a far cry from Echeverría's creed of romantic socialism was the spectacle of the Argentine people in thrall to the dictatorship of Rosas! In *El Matadero* (1838), set amidst the carnage of a slaughter-house, which is the appropriate headquarters for a gang of the tyrant's hirelings, Echeverría has also left us an unfinished novel of horrific power and still painfully relevant political symbolism.

Chile (as Bolívar had predicted) was spared the horrors of dictatorship from which the Argentine was suffering, but became the forum for heated debate on the need for 'mental emancipation'. The conservative viewpoint was voiced by the erudite Venezuelan, Andrés Bello (1781–1865), who had worked for Latin American independence in London where he had come under the influence of Mill and Bentham before being called to Chile to build up that country's educational system. There he founded the University of Chile, brought order out of the chaos of obsolete colonial legislation by drawing up a new legal code, composed treatises of grammar and orthography to prevent the degeneration of local speech from standard Spanish, and wrote a series of works on literary criticism and philosophy. He also composed long poems in the neo-classical style; the best known of these is rather forbiddingly entitled *To the Agriculture of the Torrid Zone* (1826), indicating that it was not so much nature herself, but what man had done with nature, that deserved to be sung. Bello was a great organiser and disseminator of learning in the spirit of the Enlightenment. He was fully aware that political emancipation could only be completed by mental emancipation, but he differed from many contemporaries on the importance which he attached to the Spanish heritage for the gestation of the Latin American mind. The best elements in the Spanish past, he warned, must not be thrown away in the eagerness to build an independent future. At a time when it was fashionable to deride Spain's achievement and blame the former metropolis for all the ills of the present, Bello stoutly championed the principle of continuity. He pointed out that the very qualities of vigour, endurance, and self-sacrifice by which the Creoles had achieved their independence were Spanish qualities; and independent Latin America could only find her own path into the future if she continued to draw sustenance from the culture in which she had been nurtured.

The balance and moderation of Bello's views seemed contemptibly insipid to more ardent spirits, and were challenged by one of the master's own pupils in a famous address to the University of Chile on the Social Influence of the *Conquista* and the Colonial System. José Victorino Lastarria (1817–1888), in a fiery restatement of the Black Legend, dismissed Spain's achievement in the New World as 'three hundred years of gloom', and the schools and universities she had established as 'monuments of imbecility'. Law had been nothing but codified tyranny, officials had thought only of feathering their own nests, trade and useful arts had been despised as degrading, and religion itself had been misused to bolster up the whole system of despotism. Chilean society was still labouring under the frightful burden of the past, and Lastarria called on his hearers to 'destroy completely the resistance offered by the old Spanish system embodied in our society'. This theme Lastarria continued to elaborate until the end of his life. Where Bello had stressed the good qualities which the descendants of the colonists carried in their blood, Lastarria was concerned with their inherited weaknesses and defects. He saw the liberty of the individual as the goal towards which society must strive. Spain had denied that goal, especially to the *mestizos* who were scorned and ignored. If the Creoles aspired to real freedom they must then wholly repudiate their Spanish past.

Another Chilean thinker, Francisco Bilbao (1823–1865), went even further than Lastarria. He saw America as a battlefield in which the spirit of the Middle Ages was engaged in mortal combat with the spirit of modern progress. In the United States the modern spirit was victorious; not so in the 'Disunited States' of the South. The heart of the medieval spirit, of the Spanish heritage, was the Church. Catholicism, since it denied the sovereignty of the people and the primacy of human reason, was irreconcilable with the Republicanism which the ex-colonies had chosen as their form of government. 'This is the dualism of South America, a dualism which will destroy us if we do not make one of the two propositions prevail', he wrote. 'Either Catholicism triumphs, and monarchy and theocracy rule America, or Republicanism triumphs with free reason and the religion of law dominating the conscience of every man.' These views, expressed in the revolutionary manifesto *Sociabilidad Chilena* (1844), were considered as seditious and blasphemous, and their author was forced into exile. Given the still conservative state of the society established in power by the 'revolution' of independence, Bilbao's voice could never be more than a cry in the wilderness. But what a voice it was, with its passionate invocations to the great principles of Liberty, Equality, Goodness, and Justice, and his faith that America must look to herself for her own salvation! 'Europe cannot civilise herself, and yet she wants to civilise us!' Nor did Bilbao shrink from propounding practical remedies. He advocated such measures as the creation of an international tribunal and an American University, the abolition of customs dues, a common citizenship, a Federal Congress with legislative power, joint planning for reforms—all dangerous and visionary proposals in his day, but some of them now already accomplished and others on the way to realisation.

'*Civilisation and barbarism*'

One of those who took vigorous part in Chilean polemics, siding with Lastarria and branding the admirable Bello as 'anachronistic', was an Argentine exile who was destined to become President of his country and one of its most famous writers. Domingo Faustino Sarmiento (1811–1888) had been born in the Andean foothills and grew up in the years of anarchy which followed the wars of independence. Bands of fierce *gauchos* roamed the Argentine *pampa* taking the law into their own hands and terrorising the towns. One day he witnessed the entry of the local *caudillo*, Facundo Quiroga, at the head of his barbarous horde. It was, he afterwards wrote, 'a sudden revelation of all the ills which tormented my country —barbarism'. The *gaucho* bands appeared to him as 'the source and symbol of the wretchedness, the savagery, and the poverty of the people'. He reached the conclusion that they could only be redeemed by education and the spread of enlightened reforms. To this end he devoted his life as a writer and politician, returning to Argentina to assist in the overthrow of the dictator

Rosas and using his high office to endow his country with the schools which he believed would be the best foundation for its greatness.

The book which is at once the most famous and the most interesting of Sarmiento's vast output is significantly entitled *Civilización y Barbarie* (1845), though it is more popularly known as *Facundo*, after the *caudillo* who made such a vivid impression on his youthful imagination. *Facundo* is an extraordinary compound of biography, contemporary history, political diatribe, sociological interpretation, and essay in national psychology. It is a prophet's vision of his country, the revelation of its ills, and a call to its redemption. Sarmiento himself described it as 'a chunk of rock hurled at the head of a tyrant!' The book is composed of three parts; the first comprises a description of the unique geographical and sociological character of the *pampa* and of the *gauchos* who inhabit it—a superb portrait gallery of now largely vanished national types; the second part relates the life of Facundo Quiroga; and the third leads from an account of the *caudillo*'s crimes to an indictment of dictatorship on the national scale. Quiroga's career was ended by his murder, but—as Sarmiento declares—'Facundo is not dead; he lives on in popular tradition, in Argentine politics and revolution, in Rosas, his heir and fulfilment. His soul has passed into that more finished, more perfect mould, and that which in him was mere instinct, embryo, and trend, has been converted by Rosas into system, form, and purpose.'

Sarmiento's thesis is that the lawlessness from which Argentina and much of Latin America was suffering stemmed not so much from the Spanish heritage which so obsessed thinkers like Lastarria and Bilbao as from the brutalising effect of the primitive environment. This had produced, he wrote, 'two diverse civilisations, one Spanish, European, civilised; the other barbarous, American, native almost'. The latter was the breeding-ground for *caudillos* like Facundo, on the local scale, and Rosas, on the national scale. Now the country or *campo*, in its Latin American context, has nothing in common with the homely English countryside, the setting for picturesque *Cranfords* or for the BBC's Archer family. The *pampa*, Sarmiento declares, resembles the steppes of Asia in its immensity and solitude; 'society has vanished entirely; there remains only the feudal family, isolated and turned in upon itself, and where men do not live in society, all form of government is rendered impossible'. The cities are too few and too puny to tame the *pampa*; 'the desert is never far removed from them; it hems them in and presses upon them . . . The evil which afflicts the Argentine Republic is its vast extent.' Between the *gauchos* and other men lies an unbridgeable gulf. 'Implacable is the hatred which civilised men inspire in them. They seem to be two entirely different societies, two nations alien to each other.' The wars of independence did not bring them together; if the *gauchos* had fought in them, it was only out of natural bellicosity. 'To break free from the authority of the King was welcome to them, for it meant a breaking free from authority in general.' The upshot was a conflict in two stages: first, the campaign waged by the cities against Spain; secondly, the war waged by the *caudillos* against the cities. As Sarmiento wrote: 'the cities triumphed over Spain, and the *caudillos* over the cities. . . . We wanted unity in civilisation and liberty; we have been given unity in barbarism and slavery.'

Sarmiento's thesis of civilisation and barbarism may be applied to other parts of Latin America besides Argentina. Venezuela, for instance, has its counterpart to the *pampa* in the *llanos*, the vast stretch of rolling plains, still wilder and more primitive, since they are cut off from the sea by mountain ranges. The *llanero* inhabits a land even harsher than that of the *gaucho*, for it lies nearer the equator and is traversed by alligator-infested rivers. The discovery of oil has brought modernity to the cities but has been slow to bring enlightenment to the *campo*. It is ironical that in Caracas, the home of the Liberator, dictators have ruled longer and more absolutely than in most other capitals of Latin America. It was not until the middle of the present century that they have given place to democratically elected Presidents, the first of whom was also the country's most famous novelist. In *Doña Bárbara* (1929), his best known book, Rómulo Gallegos (1884–) depicts a woman who, brutalised by the harsh life of the *llanos*, rules her ranch like some robber baron of the dark ages until she is finally mastered by the hero and heroine, who represent the civilised values of the city. Brazil has its own epic of rural fanaticism in da Cunha's famous *Os Sertões*.[1] In other countries it is the tropical forest rather than the plain which is the brutalising environment, as the Colombian writer José Eustasio Rivera (1889–1928) has so powerfully shown in his novel *La Vorágine* (1924).

In recent years some parts of Latin America have seen an intensification of this basic dichotomy between city and *campo*. The latter continues to invade the towns in search of at least some of the material benefits which industrialisation offers. The *campo* 'hems them in and presses upon them', fringing the larger urban centres with enormous and appalling shanty settlements. But the brilliant antitheses of *Facundo* no longer wholly match the context of today. 'Barbarism', as we can see

1. See p. 140

from books such as *Quarto de Despejo* (1960), the diary kept by the Negress Carolina Maria de Jesus in the slums of São Paulo, may also breed those who are ready to make the most heroic sacrifices in their aspirations towards a more civilised life. Violence and brutality may as readily dominate a social élite, as the Peruvian Mario Vargas Llosa shows in his novel of life in a military college, *La Ciudad y los Perros* (1962).

The idealisation of the gaucho

Sarmiento himself recognised later in life that (thanks largely to his own efforts to promote education, immigration, and material progress) the portrait of his country could no longer be painted in the crude colours of his early pallet. In a preface to an English translation of *Facundo* he admitted that 'we cannot always tell from the facts on which side barbarism lies, where political passions are aroused in youthful nations'. A similar view was expounded in *La Política Liberal bajo la Tiranía* (1873) by José Manuel Estrada, the first occupant of the chair of Civic Instruction which Sarmiento had founded. Estrada, whilst offering an interpretation broadly similar to Sarmiento's, saw his nation's dichotomy in terms of intellectuals and masses, rather than of civilisation and barbarism, and kept some severe strictures for the *clase pensadora*. More recently, Ricardo Rojas (1882–1957), who devoted a massive biography to the Prophet of the Pampa and saw himself as continuing and, where necessary, rectifying the work of the master, carries matters still further. Sarmiento's thesis, he argues, is etymologically correct, but applicable only to the classical world where cities were indeed the nuclei of civilisation. In America the reality is different; there they were founded as strong-points for the conquest of the interior, and became 'centres exotic, hostile, and barbarous in origin, since the newcomers were alien to the land'. As the countries of the New World developed distinctive characters of their own, the cities remained 'survivors of the Spanish tradition'. Foreign immigrants and capital made of the ports 'factories for economic exploitation at the expense of the agriculture and the indigenous population'. The result, according to Rojas, has been that 'in the present state of our country, it is the *campo* which is the seat of civilisation on account of its valiant labour which sustains the cities, the moral health of those who live in it, and because its landscape and traditions are the inspiration of our nascent art, whereas the cities are parasites of bureaucracy, commerce, slothful sensuality, cosmopolitan rootlessness—in short, of barbarism. The terms of the problems posed by Sarmiento have been reversed.'

The theme of civilisation and barbarism has evoked the counter-myth of the *gaucho* as the symbol of liberty and the epitome of the nation's virtues. The *gauchos* of Uruguay had played a notable part in the wars of independence, and a Uruguayan writer, Bartolomé Hidalgo (1788–1822), adopted *gaucho* dialect in his political pamphleteering with some success. Hilario Ascasubi (1807–1875), an enemy of Rosas, and Estanislao del Campo (1834–1880), with his amusing if artificial gauchesque version of the Faust legend, did much the same in Argentina. The Argentine man of letters José Hernández (1834–1886) also set out to write his famous poem *Martín Fierro* (1872) in the spirit of a political tract, as a protest against the press-ganging of *gauchos* for the border wars against the Indians. Fierro, the noble anarchist of the *pampas*, relates his story in pithy, vivid verse; he tells of the untrammelled life before the coming of 'civilisation', the suffering and injustice brought upon him by the war, the tavern brawls and brutal knife-fight, his pursuit and flight, and the refuge finally sought by the outcast amongst the wild Indians. A few years later, when Sarmiento (whom he hated) had left the Presidency, Hernández published his sequel, *La Vuelta de Martín Fierro* (1879), in which his hero, though nostalgically remembering the days of freedom, comes to terms with 'civilisation'. Hernández was concerned with correcting the false picture of the *gaucho* as presented by the political pamphleteers. So well did he succeed, and so thoroughly did he steep himself in the authentic *gaucho* spirit, that the epic adventures of his Martín Fierro not only fixed the image of the *gaucho* in the imagination of his literate compatriots for all time, but speedily took a commanding place in the folklore of the *gauchos* themselves.

Martín Fierro has come to be regarded as one of the most original, the most genuinely 'American' work of the creole mind. Yet even here the Spanish strains of ancestry can surely be discerned. The Argentine *payador*, thrumming his guitar and reciting his ballads to his unlettered audience of the *pampa*, is the descendant of the medieval *juglar* with his repertoire of *romances*. And it is curious to note that it was a Spanish writer, Miguel de Unamuno, who discovered the literary merits of Hernández' poem and recited its verses with enthusiasm to his students at Salamanca when it was still unacclaimed in its land of origin. And can we not see that the *poncho* cast about the shoulders of *Don Segundo Sombra* (1926), the undoubted masterpiece amongst the many *gaucho* novels which came to be written, is in reality no less than the mantle of the immortal Don Quixote? Each, in his wanderings, belongs in spirit to a bygone age. By the time that Ricardo Güiraldes (1886–1927) wrote his novel, the *pampa* had been tamed by railway and barbed wire. The *gaucho* had become a hired hand or a half-degenerate anachronism. Only the irrepressible Don Segundo refused to conform, still restlessly roaming the *pampa* and attracting by the archaic integrity of his mysterious personality the lad who tells his story and himself learns to live the hard *gaucho* life. The boy grows to manhood and is reclaimed by civilisation whilst his old friend vanishes, like the shadow which is his name, into the immensity of the *pampa*.

Martín Fierro and *Don Segundo Sombra* are the twin peaks of a genre which, from the modest origins of *gaucho* 'westerns', has established itself as a distinctive branch of literature. Its popularity corresponds to the psychological needs of an increasingly urban population. Jorge Luis Borges, the distinguished Argentine novelist who moves in the very different world of ironic and scholarly fantasy, has pointed out that by the reading of this *gaucho* literature 'the civilised inhabitants of the modern cities of the River Plate now compensate themselves for what they have missed; the physical dangers, the barbarous duels with flashing knives, the nights spent in the open air with the saddle as pillow, the drunkenness, rape and violent death'.

From romanticism to 'modernismo'

Whilst this cult of the *gaucho* was developing in the lands of the *pampa*, Romanticism remained in vogue in most parts of Latin America. Romanticism was less a formal movement than a mood, whose manifestations ranged from the youthful poems of Echeverría, and even of the analytical Alberdi, to the early novels on indigenous themes which we have studied in a previous chapter. In poetry its most notable achievement is probably *Tabaré* (1888) by the Uruguayan Juan Zorrilla de San Martín (1855–1931), a poem of epic proportions but mainly lyrical inspiration treating of the typically romantic theme of lovers separated by differences of race and culture. In prose the best known example is the novel *María* (1867) by the Colombian Jorge Isaacs (1837–1895)—an elegy of youthful love and death, redeemed from insipidity by a certain ingenuous integrity of sentiment and a perceptive feeling for its American setting. At the height of *María*'s popularity, and in the same year as the publication of *Tabaré*, there appeared *Azul*, a volume of highly original poems and prose passages by the young Nicaraguan Rubén Darío (1867–1916). It marked the advent of a new portent—*modernismo*.

What was so modern about *modernismo*? The movement was an amalgam of many -isms: symbolism, parnassianism, exoticism. Latin American writers had always been derivative. The young poets of *modernismo* carried this tendency to unprecedented lengths. They sought their models not only in the many-sided genius of France, but in fields as diverse as classical antiquity, Scandinavian mythology, Shakespeare, Buddhism, the pre-Raphaelites. Eclecticism, practised in such a thoroughgoing manner, became in itself a title to originality. None but Latin Americans could have gone about it so wholeheartedly; 'partly, it was because of our close material and spiritual commerce with the different nations of the world', wrote Darío, 'but chiefly because the new generation of [Latin] American writers is imbued with an immense thirst for progress and a lively enthusiasm'. This led them not merely to imitate, but to absorb and adapt, thereby enriching the language with a new range of resources which profoundly influenced stylists like Azorín and Valle Inclán in Spain itself. As one critic has put it: '*Modernismo* was Spanish America's first original contribution to world literature.'

The alchemy could hardly have worked without the genius of the movement's acknowledged master. The fastidious artistry of the masterpieces which followed—*Prosas Profanas* (1896) and *Cantos de Vida y Esperanza* (1905)—remained unsullied by the careless bohemianism of the poet's life. Darío left his native Nicaragua to seek his living first in Chile, then in Paris. Fame came to him, and he briefly enjoyed the accolade of being appointed his country's diplomatic representative in Spain. The significance of the appointment was symbolic. The exoticism which had been the extreme expression of the striving for 'mental emancipation' had at length led to a rediscovery of the precious cultural heritage of Spain—a heritage which Darío's own genius was in turn to enrich. And not Spain's alone, but also that of the America which Spain had done so much to fashion and which the poet saw threatened by the materialist greed of the Anglo-Saxon north. In poems such as *To Theodore Roosevelt* and *The Song to Argentina* (1914) the escapist reveals himself as now passionately *engagé*. The path which leads from aestheticism towards some political or social goal has often been trodden in Latin America, not always to the advantage of the poetic muse. The Peruvian César Vallejo (1892–1938) and, in our own time, the supremely gifted Chilean Pablo Neruda (1904–) are perhaps the most famous poets to espouse the Communist creed.

Cuba and Martí

There was one corner of the Spanish-speaking world which had not succeeded in freeing itself from the preoccupations of an earlier generation. Cuba and Puerto Rico, thanks to their position as Caribbean islands easily accessible to Spanish reinforcements, had failed to gain political independence at the same time as Spain's colonies on the mainland. Cuba's history throughout the nineteenth-century thus continued to be dominated by the issue of whether the island would become independent, and, if so, by which means, or whether it should merely aim at achieving some form of autonomy. The question was complicated by Cuba's proximity to the United States, and the attraction felt by some Cuban landowners for the economic vigour of the northern republic and particularly for the outlook of her slave-owning South. Delay in freeing herself from Spanish rule, however, might also have brought Cuba some advantage in the long run. If the other colonies had suffered through winning independence before they had attained the 'mental emancipation' necessary to reconcile liberty with order, could not Cuba at least learn that lesson? It was a challenge which inspired a dedicated series of educationalists and political thinkers: Father Félix Varela (1787–1853), José Antonio Saco (1797–1879), José de la Luz (1800–1862), and Enrique José Varona (1849–1933). It also inspired the Puerto Rican Eugenio María de Hostos (1839–1903) to devote a lifetime in exile to tireless educational work and campaigning in favour of the independence of his homeland. But Spain showed no disposition to be talked into giving her last colonies their freedom. Puerto Rico found herself liberated from Spain only to be annexed by the United States, whilst Cuba had to pay for her independence with bitter bloodshed and a legacy of violence and instability. For all the labours of her *pensadores* and political mentors, she was no better able than the other independent republics to harmonise personal liberties with order, and national prosperity with social justice.

The greatest figure to emerge in Cuba's struggle for independence was a writer who ended by exchanging the pen for the sword and crowned the eloquence of his words with the sacrifice of his life in battle. José Martí (1853–1895), the son of a Spanish soldier who had served and then settled in Cuba, was imprisoned when only sixteen for his youthful writings in favour of Cuban independence. Most of his life was spent in exile in Spain, Central America, and particularly in the United States, where he devoted himself to prolific literary work and to the political organisation of other Cuban exiles. 'The poem of 1810 was left unfinished,' he declared, 'and I wished to write its final verse.' His labours culminated in the raising of an expeditionary force which made an important contribution to the island's liberation from Spanish rule in 1898. He himself was killed in action three years earlier.

Martí's writings, scattered mainly through the pages of numerous newspapers and journals, cover an immense range: poetry, economics, reportage, children's books, philosophy, art and literary criticism, political essays and manifestoes. They constitute a rich quarry from which later writers and politicians have tended to extract what most takes their fancy. But underlying the diversity and sometimes inconsistency of his work there are certain well-marked themes which together form the framework of his ideology. Though national independence was his constant concern, Martí ranks as a Latin American rather than a narrowly Cuban writer, for he passionately believed that Cuba's cause was Latin America's cause. 'In Cuba', he wrote, 'we are not fighting just for the good of the island; we are fighting to safeguard the independence of all Latin America by safeguarding our own.' He was profoundly aware that the Latin American countries were bound together by a common culture and history, and that what happened to any one of them must affect them all. The development of Latin America, he held, had been warped by the blind imitation of foreign models. 'In America, the good ruler is not the man who knows how the French and Germans are ruled, but who understands the different elements which make up his own country.' Latin Americans should learn to study and appreciate their native heritage; it was more important for them to know about the Incas than about the Greeks. Too often they 'go out into the world wearing French or Yankee spectacles, and aspire to govern a country of which they are quite ignorant'. Governments formed with so little relation to the real needs and nature of their countries were peculiarly liable to be overthrown by the curse of Latin American politics, the brutal *caudillos*, for those at least had an intuitive understanding of their own people.

The *caudillo* represents the perverted, self-seeking, tyrannical form of leadership; Latin America needs the disinterested leadership of truly great men like Bolívar, San Martín, and Hidalgo who genuinely championed the cause of the oppressed. 'A man does not make a nation,' he wrote, 'but the nation, at the hour of its birth may find its vibrant, triumphant incarnation in a Man.' Such heroic leaders must be held in special esteem, 'and the errors they commit forgiven them, since the good they did was greater than their faults'. But the people need to be constantly on their guard lest their leaders betray them by an abuse of power; 'the ruler who proves false to the programme for which he has been elected is a thief of office. ... Those who wage wars out of ambition, or to enslave other people, or to increase their own power, are not heroes but criminals.' For, in the last analysis, 'the greatness of nations rests on the independence of individuals' and not on the power of the *caudillo*. Martí is the tireless champion of the underdog, quick to denounce all those who abuse their power, whether as political tyrants or heartless entrepreneurs. His voice is that of a romantic Liberalism rather than of a Socialism which he distrusted as a 'future slavery' imposed by an 'autocratic officialdom' and shaped by the 'the pride and hidden rage of ambitious men who, in order to rise in the world and be able to climb on to other people's shoulders, pretend to be ardent defenders of the helpless'.

The originality of Martí lies in his conviction that 'the future must be conquered with clean hands', and that a better social order can be built only by those whom he calls 'fanatics of love' and not by the 'fanatics of hate'. In writing of Karl Marx, he declared that he deserved honour for siding with the poor, but censure for stirring up passion and hatred. Martí referred to the Social Revolutionaries as 'our angry brothers' whose violence might pervert the justice they professed to serve, and he had words of warning for those workers 'who do not understand that justice is more than the mere satisfaction of their desires', and that 'to be wretched is not necessarily to be right'. The absence of hatred and bitterness is a central feature of Martí's writings as of his own personality, and it is this which has earned him the name of The Apostle by which he is widely known throughout Latin America. Martí returns constantly to the theme that 'the only law of Authority is Love . . . Mankind is composed of two sorts of men—those who love and create, and those who hate and destroy'. Yet he is no pious sentimentalist. 'Look into the hearts of men and you will shudder', he wrote. 'Whenever I gaze on men I draw back as before an abyss.' Nor, despite his mystical faith in the virtues of love and self-sacrifice, can he be ranked as a conventional Christian writer. He saw in his own country a Church identified with the repressive authority of Spain and indifferent to its mission of succouring the humble and oppressed. 'Christianity has perished at the hands of Catholicism' is a characteristic Martían apothegm.

Martí spent the most fruitful years of his life in the United States, and few foreigners have written of the republic of Washington, Jefferson, and Lincoln with greater insight and admiration. But this admiration was tempered with caution. Between Anglo-Saxon and Latin America, so different in the nature of their genius and in material strength, he held that there should be friendship and mutual respect but no formal bonds, for union between them could be only 'the union between the condor and the lamb'. He watched with misgiving the new expansionist vigour of the northern republic and greeted with scepticism the first International American Conference held in Washington in 1889, noting with concern the contemptuous references often made to the Latin Americans by United States journalists and even statesmen, with their brash assumption that the Anglo-Saxons were a superior race. Though often cited as a precursor of Pan-Americanism, Martí was in some respects more an advocate of neutralism. He feared that Cuba might free herself from Spain only to be absorbed by a United States avid for fresh markets and profitable new fields for investment. 'Economic union will lead to political union', he warned. 'The country which buys lays down the law; the country which sells has to obey. A balance must be struck in a country's trade, if its independence is to be preserved. A nation which wants to die sells to a single country; a nation which wants to live sells to more than one. Excessive influence by one country on the trade of another becomes political influence.' To this theme Martí frequently returned, urging the Cubans to resist the temptation to sell exclusively to the United States. 'The first step a nation takes in order to establish control over another is to separate that country from others. The country which wishes to remain free must be free in its commerce. It should distribute its trade between countries of equal strength. If preference must be given to one of them, then it should go to the nation which needs it the less. The fact that we happen to live geographically near to each other does not oblige us to political union. . . . Let us be united with the rest of the world, and not just one part of it; not with just one part of it against another.' Here, in a nutshell, is the Cuban dilemma, that of all countries where a monoculture makes them vulnerable to those of stronger and more diversified economy—a dilemma from which the present political leaders of Cuba sought to escape only to fall into an even more thorough economic dependence through the sale of their sugar not to the United States but to the Soviet Union.

The northern Colossus

Martí's anti-clericalism and romantic liberalism are in the tradition of the earlier fathers of Latin American independence, though he is less naively unreserved in his enthusiasm for what was fast becoming the Colossus of the North. Alberdi, Sarmiento, Bilbao, and others had been convinced that the example of the United States had much to offer their own countries. Sarmiento wrote copiously and enthusiastically about the northern republic, which he particularly admired for its system of popular education, and ended one of his books with the exhortation to his countrymen to make of their land another United States. Bilbao proclaimed that the cause of North America's greatness was to be found in its spirit of industrious Puritanism, the antithesis of the Catholicism which he blamed for the retrograde Spanish mentality. Alberdi drew inspiration from the Constitution of the United States for his *Bases para la Organización política de Argentina* (1852), which in turn shaped the new Argentine constitution drafted after the fall of Rosas. It was Alberdi who coined the watchword *gobernar es poblar*—to govern is to populate—and declared that for undeveloped countries such as his own, 'a minister of state who does not double the population every ten years is wasting his time in trifles and frivolities'. The spectacular development of Argentina in the second half of the nineteenth century justified the creed of immigration, education, and progress preached by such men as Sarmiento and Alberdi. The mighty stream of immigrants from Europe was composed largely of Italians, and their coming has added a permanent flavour to the national life. Alberdi would have preferred to see more Anglo-Saxon settlers, since he believed that they would bring the qualities of political maturity needed if democratic institutions were to take proper root. 'Liberty', he wrote, 'is like a machine which, for its proper functioning, needs not only steam but engineers of English origin as well. . . . A country without the English is like a wood without birds.' It was the Anglo-Saxon immigrants in North America, with their spirit of practical progress and civil liberties, who were converting the ex-colonies into the awakening Colossus.

The admiration felt by many of the *próceres* for the United States may seem surprising today, when strident anti-American feeling is so prevalent in Latin America. The sentiment is, more properly, one of love-hate; much of the earlier admiration, if now tinged with envy and fear at the present overpowering material power of the Colossus, may still be found beneath the crust of antipathy. A century ago, the other facet of this ambivalent attitude was more in evidence. Though the United States had not in fact made much practical contribution to the cause of Latin American emancipation, it was felt that both parts of the hemisphere had chosen parallel paths to national independence. Washington, and later Abraham Lincoln, were revered as symbols of continental grandeur. Spain was the enemy; the Anglo-Saxon spirit was hailed as being in obvious contradiction to the stultifying heritage of Spanish mentality. Anglo-Saxon attitudes and institutions were commended, if not really assimilated, as assisting the process of 'mental emancipation'. But as the nineteenth century wore on, the mood changed. Spain ceased to be a threat. The Spanish heritage came to be increasingly recognised, as Bello and a few others had always recognised it to be, as an essential element in the emergent personality of Latin America. To become another United States was something not only beyond the power but also (except for the emulation of purely material achievements) totally beyond the wishes of the Latin Americans. Enhanced status had wrought a change of mood in the United States as well. Far from practising liberty in silence, as Alberdi had declared, they had seized vast tracts of Mexican territory and were intervening as they saw fit in the Caribbean and Central America. Theodore Roosevelt seemed to have perverted the Monroe Doctrine into an imperialist creed giving a free hand to the Yankees against their weaker neighbours.

The Latin American revulsion against the growing influence of the northern Colossus is reflected in the work of the Uruguayan *littérateur*, José Enrique Rodó (1871–1917). Whether or not he is the profound thinker and 'magician of Spanish prose' claimed by his admirers, Rodó is certainly a fastidious stylist and master of the essay form. *Motivos de Proteo* (1909), his most substantial and probably his best work, is really a vast mosaic made up of parables, prose-poems, anecdotes, and meditations on the spiritual essence of man's nature and the need for each individual to preserve it from contamination and to find constant renewal for it. The plea had already been made in Rodó's slighter but more famous *Ariel* (1900), a monologue in which the sage bids farewell to his pupils and exhorts them to eschew vulgarity, and to cultivate nobility of mind, good taste, and delicacy of feeling, thus giving to America the spiritual leadership which the continent needs but cannot expect from the prosperous and industrious philistines—'I admire them, though I have no love for them'—of the North. This Olympian advice is delivered in an elevated style appropriate to the theme. Of all Latin American writers, none is less easy for the English or American reader to appreciate than Rodó. It is not so much that we resent his censure; it is rather that the unrelieved refinement, the constant allusions to Renan and Taine, and the sustained elevation of sentiment become a trifle cloying. We would gladly exchange it all for Sarmiento's 'chunk of rock' hurled at the head—even though the head be ours—of ignorance and philistinism.

Ariel achieved immense and instant popularity. Though the unflattering references to the United States had been only illustrative and not central to Rodó's theme, they were hailed as the credo of a whole generation. His thesis became over-simplified into the crude antithesis between Caliban-North America and Ariel-Latin America, Materialism versus Idealism.

For educated Latin Americans, in the words of one of their writers who had misgivings about its ultimate effect, Rodó's myth provided 'the justification of their racial characteristics, the compensation for their practical backwardness, the claim to spiritual superiority over the Titan of the North'.

The need for 'economic emancipation'

If Rodó stressed the dangers of spiritual contagion from the Yankees' allegedly materialistic attitude to life, other Latin Americans were more concerned with its economic consequences. We have noted the misgivings expressed on this score by so staunch an admirer of the United States as Martí. This fear that the economic expansion of the United States would stifle the independence of Latin America was hardening into the creed of 'economic anti-imperialism' which colours much of Latin America's thinking today. Though formulated in Marxist terms by Lenin, who saw in the Argentine the classic example of a semi-colony dominated by foreign capitalist interests, the creed has indigenous roots in the Latin Americans' own quest for identity. As the Mexican philosopher Leopoldo Zea has put it: 'Formerly it was a struggle against Spain; now it is a struggle against our new mother country, the United States, for we are still a colony. It is always the same, a struggle for our independence. At one time it was a political struggle against Spain; then it was a spiritual struggle against Spain's habits and customs, and later an economic struggle against the bourgeoisie of which we are only the tools.' Political independence, mental independence, economic independence—such, in short, are the stages which many Latin Americans see as constituting their natural progression towards complete maturity.

The fathers of independence gave little attention to economic matters, although the urge for more economic freedom and a wider choice of markets had sharpened their discontent with Spanish rule. Their energies were absorbed by urgent military and political tasks. They were preoccupied with frontiers, constitutions, and civil wars. The chief problems facing them seemed to be those of political underdevelopment rather than of economic underdevelopment. The ruling class tended to belittle interest in the promotion of manufacturing, since they were landowners and in some cases slave-owners. If men like Rivadavia in Argentina and O'Higgins in Chile took some steps to encourage 'useful arts' and promote trade and development, they were still acting broadly in the spirit of Enlightened Despotism. In general, *laissez-faire* held sway, and most would have agreed with Alberdi that 'there is no better or safer way to impoverish a country than to entrust its government with the task of enriching it'; or, as the Brazilian puts it with a more tolerant cynicism, 'Our country grows by night when the politicians are asleep.' Governments were content to invite foreign merchants, artisans, and engineers to their country to help open it up as they saw fit. Foreign capital (mostly British) was welcomed to the same end. Both foreigners and their resources were regarded as indispensable allies in the struggle to replace the backwardness of the Spanish colonial regime with a more progressive order; only later, when the scale and influence of such foreign participation had become manifest, did they begin to be felt as harmful to the nation's progress and dignity.

In so far as thinkers and politicians, in the first decades of independence, felt concern at Latin America's lack of economic progress they tended to attribute it mainly to the deleterious 'Spanish heritage' or to innate racial defects. Sarmiento came to realise in later life that the environmental thesis so brilliantly developed in *Facundo* was not a sufficient explanation, at least for other parts of America, and that 'the root of the evil went deeper than the external accidents of physical environment led me to suppose'. In his rather rambling *Conflictos y Armonías de las Razas* (1883) he suggested that racial mixture was in fact the main cause, and that the Anglo-Saxons were superior, both in themselves and in their institutions. Similar conclusions were reached by another Argentine writer, Carlos Octavio Bunge (1875–1918), in his interesting but rather pedantic *Nuestra América* which appeared three years after Rodó's more polished and beguiling *Ariel.* The Bolivian writer Alcides Arguedas, whose penetrating study of Indian life we have already noted,[1] offered in his *Pueblo Enfermo* (1910) a no less pessimistic assessment of America whose 'illness' he ascribed both to its harsh physical environment and to the innate incapacity of the *mestizos*—an assessment challenged by Rodó, who countered that Latin America was not so much sick as simply young and immature. Two years later the Chilean historian Francisco Encina (1874–) published his *Nuestra Inferioridad Económica* in which his country's economic backwardness was attributed less to purely economic causes than to inherited character defects such as the prodigal get-rich-quick mentality of the Asturians or the plodding mediocrity of the Basques. Such writers, in short, turned their gaze inwards and did not shrink from the most harrowing soul-searching in their quest for the cause of Latin America's ills.

But others were persuaded that the cause was extraneous. We have seen how writers like Ricardo Rojas (who dismissed *Conflictos y Armonías de las Razas* as a 'chaotic and lamentable

1. See p. 39

book') inverted Sarmiento's thesis of the 'barbarism' of the *campo* and 'civilisation' of cities, branding the latter as alien and parasitic. In books such as Martínez Estrada's *Radiografía de la Pampa* (1933) this thesis is developed into a full-blown indictment of 'economic imperialism'. The foreign merchants and technicians who were welcomed to the Argentine did not, it is argued, really contribute to the country's wealth, but exploited its resources primarily in the foreign interest. Foreign capital organised the economy according to the requirements of the overseas markets, and not for the benefit of the population as a whole. The British-built railways, for instance, were constructed not with a view to promoting the unity and serving the economic needs of the nation, but for the purpose of carrying 'camp' produce by the quickest route to Buenos Aires and Europe, thus neglecting vast rural areas and inflating the importance of the capital. By the end of the Second World War, as elsewhere in Latin America, American capital had supplanted British in importance, and 'economic imperialism' wore a Yankee rather than a British guise. We find its role explored with considerable philosophical, sociological, and psychological sophistication in the vast output of José Ingenieros (1877–1925) and more stridently denounced in the writings of Manuel Ugarte (1878–1951). But if we would follow what promises to be the most original, influential, and constructive elaboration of the need for economic emancipation theme, we must turn to the work of another Argentinian, Dr Raul Prebisch (1901–), whose influence in the United Nations' Economic and Social Council for Latin America has given birth to a whole school of economic thought which offers both ideology and practical programmes.

This ideology, as developed in such documents as *The*

Economic Development of Latin America and its Principal Problems (1949) and *Towards a Dynamic Policy for Latin America* (1963), criticises the traditional concept of Latin America as an underdeveloped area whose function should remain that of producing food and raw material for the great industrial centres. The latter, by the operation of economic law, inevitably increase in wealth at the expense of the less developed periphery; Latin America's backwardness thus results from the international trading system with its concomitant deterioration in her terms of trade. It can be redressed only by some degree of industrialisation and the opening up of world markets to such manufactured goods as she is able to produce. Foreign capital has an important part to play in furthering her industrialisation provided it is carefully channelled and controlled at the receiving end. It follows that detailed plans need to be worked out for the development of individual countries (and this the Latin American Economic and Social Council has helped to do) and that these countries also need to work out some form of association in a Latin American Free Trade Area. Nor is it enough to aim only at the removal of external 'bottlenecks' to economic development; there are also grave internal 'bottlenecks' which must go. These are the antiquated agrarian and social systems which hamper the growth of agricultural production, prevent social mobility and the proper deployment of human resources, keeping a few very rich and the majority very poor. Agrarian and tax reforms are urgently needed both as measures of social justice and as the source for the capital accumulation which will make industrialisation possible. Whereas in the advanced countries economic development and capital formation came first and the redistribution of income later, the two processes must come together in Latin America; changes must be made in the social structure so that the obstacles to economic growth can be removed.

The ideas outlined above are gaining wide currency in Latin America; they have also won recognition abroad and influenced the thinking behind the 'Alliance for Progress' policy adopted by President Kennedy's administration. They represent a reasonable and sophisticated statement of Latin America's need for economic emancipation shorn of the xenophobic catchwords of 'economic imperialism', yet coloured by the assumption that, since the developed countries have become rich at the expense of the underdeveloped, the aid now offered the latter is no more than the repayment of a debt. By emphasising the necessity for detailed planning, they mark a significant shift away from the Latin Americans' inveterate habit of improvising, or reaching decisions on public matters as the result of personal considerations and the spur of momentary pressures rather than of objective criteria. They reflect, as Dr Prebisch puts it, 'the imperious need to consider what our past has been, what our present is, and what we should wish to make of the future, through the exercise of deliberate control over the forces of economic and social development'.

The Mexican Revolution and its impact

Sceptics may wonder whether the current concern with economic planning may not prove as illusory as the previous generations' concern with political constitutions. They might cite the most momentous event of Latin America's history during the first quarter of the present century—the Mexican Revolution—as something totally unrelated to constitution-making, planning, or theoretical preconception. It seems to run counter to Napoleon's dictum that a revolution is an idea which has found bayonets, and to the Leninist principle that a revolution cannot occur without a revolutionary ideology.

The atmosphere of confused and seemingly aimless violence which characterised the early phase of the Mexican Revolution is vividly conveyed by the famous novel of Mariano Azuela (1873–1952), *Los de Abajo* (1916). Here we see men moved by all sorts of unworthy urges in a vast conflict which they can neither comprehend nor control. The Revolution, says one character, is like a hurricane which carries you along as if you were a dead leaf; it is like a volcano in eruption, says another, who declares (before however turning tail when the shooting starts) that 'I love the volcano because it is a volcano, the Revolution, because it is a Revolution'. Azuela, like the novelists who have chronicled the two world wars, stood appalled at the senseless, haphazard wastefulness of war and its power to reduce men to the level of beasts. His hero is a peasant who rises to become a revolutionary general before he himself is killed. The stark realism of the action is unrelieved by any glimmer of the social gains brought to the country when the fighting is over; we see only the flames of destruction, not the light irradiated by the Revolution when the fires die down. It is a pessimistic, almost an anti-revolutionary novel; but it remains the most authentic picture, painted with detached artistry and fidelity of observation, of Mexico's great upheaval, 'beautiful even in its barbarism'. Even from the perspective of the present generation, Mexican writers can still view their Revolution unsentimentally. Carlos Fuentes' *La Muerte de Artemio Cruz* (1962) shows us a ruthless revolutionary general who has not remained one of the 'underdogs', but has done exceedingly well for himself out of the Revolution; yet, as his past is unravelled and his conduct probed, we are led to realise that human personality, as indeed the Revolution itself, is too complex to be judged in simple terms of black and white.

Many different attempts have been made to define the nature of the Mexican Revolution and to explain its origins. All at least agree in stressing its specifically Mexican character. It antedated the Russian Revolution and was not sparked off by any incendiary ideas from Europe. Rather was it a nationalistic reaction against European ideas as embodied in Positivism and against foreign influences dominant in the regime of Porfirio Díaz. The Revolution expressed the urge to reassert Mexican over alien values; it erupted, as the poet Octavio Paz (1914–) has put it in his perceptive essay *El Laberinto de la Soledad* (1950), 'with all the force of the revelation of our true being. . . . Thanks to the Revolution, the Mexican seeks reconciliation with his own history and origins.' Hence the exaltation of the pre-Columbian past and the Indian strain in his heritage which we have noted in an earlier chapter. And because the indigenous Mexicans were also the 'underdogs' of Azuela's title, the nationalist, Indianist revolution was equally a social revolution. The 'underdogs' moreover were not, for the most part, an urban proletariat; they were the peons and peasants who rose to demand *Tierra y Libertad*. Hence the appeal of the agrarian revolutionary leader Zapata, as we find well expressed in the narrative of *Pedro Martínez* (1964) whose experiences in the Mexican Revolution have been recorded by the American social anthropologist Oscar Lewis: 'I want guarantees for the peasants. I want the lands taken away from the *hacendados* and given to the poor, to the people. I want the land to be for the people, not for the rich. My idea is—Water, Land, and Justice.'

The Mexican Revolution was thus at one and the same time a nationalist, pro-Indian, social, and agrarian movement. Nor do these terms suffice to define it, for the Revolution made itself felt with no less striking effect in fields such as art and letters. It is significant that 1910, which saw the beginning of the political upheaval, was also the year of the great exhibition of Mexican art. The revolution in painting, revealing dramatically new techniques and sources of inspiration, reached its fullest expression in the work of the great muralists Orozco, Rivera, and Siqueiros, the two latter revolutionaries in politics as well as in art. The same year, 1910, also marks the definitive repudiation of the ivory tower aspects of *modernismo*, with the publication of the famous verses of Enrique González Martínez (1871–1952) declaring that it was high time 'to wring the neck of the Swan', the symbol of all that was most artificial and escapist in literature. But the greatest figure of this period in Mexican letters—great also, like so many other notable Latin American writers, in fields other than literature—was a man who contributed powerfully to the shaping of the new Mexico whilst paradoxically remaining in important respects quite alien to its spirit—José Vasconcelos (1881–1958).

Vasconcelos, together with the poet González Martínez, the philosopher Antonio Caso (1883–1946), the humanist Alfonso Reyes (1889–1949), and other intellectuals, formed the influential *Ateneo de la Juventud* which did so much to change the climate in which Positivism and *porfirismo* had flourished. He threw himself into the Revolution and, as Secretary for Education, headed the drive to give the Indians schools and to draw up a comprehensive new education plan for the whole country. He then stood unsuccessfully for the Presidency, became disillusioned with the Revolution, and chose to spend most of his remaining years in exile, during which time he returned to the Catholic faith and wrote the greater part of his work, including a fascinating four-volume autobiography, numerous studies in philosophy, aesthetics, and ethics, and his famous paean to Latin America's destiny, *La Raza Cósmica* (1925). Vasconcelos came to exert immense influence throughout Latin America, comparable to that of Rodó on an earlier generation. In his ideas, no less than in his public life, he remains a source of endless contradictions and controversies. Whatever is of value in his writings, assert his enemies, is not new, and whatever may be new is of no value. But to his admirers, the voice of Vasconcelos is the most authentic and prophetic voice of Latin America.

The administrator who did so much to promote the anti-Spanish creations of the muralists himself cherished a passionate faith in the greatness of the Spanish heritage. 'We shall never be great', he wrote, 'until the Spanish American feels himself to be just as Spanish as the sons of Spain.' As for the Indian, whose ancient civilisation the Revolution now acclaimed, 'he has no other gateway into the future save that of modern culture, and no road other than that which has been traced out by Latin culture'. He saw Latin America's history as an integral part of that of Spain, whose age-long conflict against Protestant England still continued under the guise of Spanish America's struggle against 'Yankee' influence. In his scorn and distrust of the United States, Vasconcelos gives his own emphatic gloss to Rodó's *arielismo*. He even advocated a form of pan-Americanism embracing Spain but excluding the United States since the latter 'represent a different expression of human history'.

For Vasconcelos, the 'Spanishness' of the Latin Americans consisted less in whatever admixture of Spanish blood they might have than in the pervasive influence of Spanish culture. He was no racist deploring the adulteration of European stock with inferior strains. On the contrary, he hailed *mestizaje* as a special glory of the Spanish heritage, and as the precious contribution which Latin America was in turn destined to make to the emergence of the *raza cósmica* of the future. The trend of evolution, he held, is towards 'the fusion of peoples and of cultures'. The Anglo-Saxons think in terms of the domination of some races by others rather than of fusion. The Latin Americans not only favour the more civilised process of miscegenation but they possess the geographical environment in which the superior synthesis could take place. 'The great civilisations began around the tropics, and the final civilisation will return to the tropics.' Just as the white man based his civilisation on the mastery of a cold climate, so the cosmic race will blossom once the more exuberant, life-giving warmth of the tropics has been brought fully under human control by modern technology, creating in the process new skills and arts (as Brazil, for instance, has begun to create its own distinctive architecture). To the process of biological blending and the mastery of the tropical climate, Latin America would also provide a third factor necessary for the emergence of the cosmic race—'the spiritual factor which must direct and consummate the extraordinary enterprise'. Here Vasconcelos' thought takes wing and becomes less easy to follow. 'The hispanic race in general,' he concludes, 'still has before it the mission of discovering new zones of the spirit, now that there are no new lands left to be discovered.' So the prophetic vision is summed up in Vasconcelos' credo that 'only the Iberian part of [our] continent possesses the spiritual, racial, and territorial factors which are required for the great enterprise of initiating humanity's universal era'.

These tremendous affirmations have brought us a long way from the Mexican Revolution. Can the latter be said to have released any of the spiritual forces which will make for the renewal of Latin America and the accomplishment of the 'great enterprise' of Vasconcelos' vision? No other part of the hemisphere, we may have noted, has chosen to follow the Mexican path. Haya de la Torre, the founder of APRA, once served as Vasconcelos' secretary and was deeply influenced by the Mexican experience, but his movement has not triumphed in Peru. Bolivia has chosen a revolutionary path of her own; Cuba, with her eyes on Moscow, another. In Mexico itself the revolutionaries have settled down to become the 'establishment', and the ruling party significantly styles itself the *Institutional* Revolutionary Party. Some frankly hold that the Revolution has not fulfilled its early promise. This is implicit in such novels as Carlos Fuentes' *La Región más Transparente* (1958) with its evocation of the feverish aimlessness of post-revolutionary Mexican society, and also in the social documentaries of Oscar Lewis, whose *Children of Sánchez* (1961) reveals both the wretched material conditions in which many Mexicans still live and also their lack of faith in politics as a means of bettering them. Octavio Paz has shrewdly summed up the scope and limitation of his country's achievement as follows: 'The Revolution was, first, a discovery of our own selves, a return to our origins; then a search and striving for synthesis, but without success. Failing to assimilate our tradition and offer us a new nostrum it finally ended in compromise. The Revolution proved unable to relate its redeeming and explosive force to a world vision, nor could the Mexican mind resolve the conflict between the inadequacy of our traditions and our need of the universal.' This verdict is perhaps a little too severe. None of Spain's former colonies has, after all, gone further in evolving its own distinctive ethos, and the mind of modern Latin America still bears the indelible imprint of Mexico's experience.

4
The World of Brazil

In our account of Latin America and its *pensadores* we have so far made only passing reference to the great country which comprises nearly half of its land-mass and a third of its population. Differing in language, racial composition, and in many aspects of its natural environment, culture, and history, Brazil's development has run parallel to that of the Spanish American countries only in the broadest sense. We see the same groping towards national identity, the same slow gestation of a mind in the making; but the personality which begins to emerge is distinct from that of Spanish America.

The Portuguese made their first settlements along the coastal fringe of the vast land. This fringe was divided up into fiefs known as *capitânias* or captaincies donated to Portuguese nobles who were expected to open them up on their own account, much as Spain left matters to the enterprise of her *conquistadores*. But in Brazil there was no concerted march inland, no spectacular overthrow of an Aztec or Inca empire, for the land was mostly primeval forest or inhospitable brushwood *sertão*, and the inhabitants were few and extremely primitive. Colonisation was the work of settlers who gained their livelihood first from felling the brazilwood which gave the new land its name, then from plantations of sugar-cane. Large numbers of Negro slaves were imported from Africa to work these, and the colony's characteristic social and economic unit soon became the large, stoutly built house of the planter, with its adjacent slave-quarters—a house which was 'at one and the same time a fortress, a bank, a cemetery, a hospital, a school, and a house of charity giving shelter to the aged, the widow and the orphan'. If some Brazilian historians tend to dwell on the patriarchal character of the master-and-slave relationship (and the records contain no lack of evidence of its harsher side) there can be no doubt that it produced a distinctive society, well adapted to the tropical environment, in which the disparate elements of European, Indian, and Negro were mellowed, and to a certain extent fused, by a gradual process of miscegenation.

Whilst this sedentary, slave-based society was developing around Bahia and along the edge of the great 'bulge' of Brazil in the north-east, a different and more dynamic process was at work further south round the nucleus which grew into the great city of São Paulo, now the fastest growing city in the world. The energetic and enterprising character which distinguishes the present inhabitants of these parts is said to derive from their formidable ancestors who, in the early seventeenth century, began to send out expeditions into the unexplored hinterland. These *bandeirantes* organised themselves in para-military companies under the flag or *bandeira* of their chosen captain. The main objective of these bold and ruthless explorers was, in the words of an eighteenth-century writer, the capture of Indians 'whose enslavement they value even above gold; and for this reason they went on discovering and settling the far interior of Brazil, and in this way originated the discoveries of the mines'. To this breed of belated *conquistadores*, themselves of *mestizo* stock, Brazil owes the successive discoveries of gold, emeralds, and diamonds, the founding of the townships of the 'General Mines'—the modern state of Minas Gerais—and the opening of important new chapters in the story of Brazil's economic and demographic growth.

Though Portugal was for more than half a century under the Spanish Crown, she differed from Spain in the nature and methods of her colonisation, as the Portuguese *conquistador* or coloniser differed from his Spanish counterpart. 'The Portuguese coloniser', writes an American scholar, 'had a good deal less race consciousness than the Spanish *conquistador*, and he was far from being so stern in his Catholic orthodoxy.' The racial amalgam which resulted from his interbreeding with native or slave women was compounded of European, Indian, and Negro, and not, as in Spanish America, of Indian and European alone. This African strain has given a special flavour to Brazilian culture which is perhaps most marked in its folklore and music. Another important element in the life of the young colony was the 'new Christians' or Jews. They played a vital part as middlemen in the development of the sugar industry, and also made substantial contributions to letters and learning. Bento Teixeira Pinto, author of the epic *Prosopopéa* (1601), the first poem in Portuguese to treat of American themes, Ambrósio Fernandes Brandão, to whom is attributed the *Diálogos das Grandezas do Brasil* (1618), a survey of Brazil's vast natural resources which has some sharp words about 'the negligence and lack of industry of its inhabitants' who fail to develop them, and Antônio José da Silva (1705–1739), victim of the Inquisition and author of satirical plays which won popularity in Portugal, were all 'new Christians'.

Although towns such as Bahia, Olinda, and Recife soon attained a fair degree of wealth and distinction, Brazilian society was predominantly rural and the towns never approached the splendour of Spain's centres of viceregal power. Nor did Portugal permit the establishment in her colony of a university or even a printing press. Culturally and intellectually, as well as administratively and economically, Brazil was kept closely linked to the mother country. But the new land, with the exuberance and strangeness of its tropical life and the immense scale of its untamed nature, began, from the onset of colonisation, to impose its own pattern. The Portuguese language was enriched with a new vocabulary appropriate to the flora and fauna and the peculiar mode of life of the New World, and was gradually modified in structure and pronunciation by the coloured population who spoke it. Men of other European nations, particularly the French and the Dutch, attempted to secure permanent footholds in the new land. The prolonged struggle to expel them, in which the colonists had often to rely on their own resources rather than on help from overseas, did much to strengthen the nascent awareness of nationhood. Such cultural features as the intruders had succeeded in implanting were absorbed in time into the mainstream of Brazilian development.

The colonial period

If the two most remarkable literary figures of Spanish America's colonial past had been a Mexican nun and a Peruvian rake, the outstanding names of Portuguese America for the same period were those of the Jesuit father Antônio Vieira (1608–1697) (whom Sor Juana Inés engaged in controversy) and the dissolute satirist of Bahia, Gregório de Matos (1633–1696). The latter indeed shares certain similarities with Caviedes. Both drew from the same vein of corrosive satire and merciless raillery;

both paid in penury and disgrace for the frailty of their flesh and the ferocity of their tongue. But the Brazilian was reared in relative luxury and received the best education of his day in Portugal. Yet one thing he never learned—the art of flattery; nor even the prudent practice of silence. The fools that others suffered gladly enough he lambasted in verses too libellously mordant to be published in his lifetime but highly esteemed by connoisseurs of polished vituperation. *Boca do inferno,* his contemporaries dubbed him. His modern admirers laud him as 'the first native voice to be heard in Brazilian literature' and as representing 'the revolt of bourgeois good sense against the ridiculous and childish pretensions of the gentry'. But it would be a mistake to see in this dissolute genius (who ended his days in due repentance) an early paladin of social and national reform. If he lashed out at 'the rascals from Portugal', he had no less harsh words for the *mulattoes* and Negroes who composed the broad substratum of colonial society.

A striking contrast is offered by the personality and career of Antônio Vieira. For much of the seventeenth century this famous Jesuit remained at the centre of its momentous events. Thanks to his letters, his reports, and above all to the vehement eloquence of his sermons, he came to acquire an extraordinary influence, particularly with King João IV, the first independent monarch after Portugal had regained her freedom from Spain. His critics accuse him of defeatism in the struggle against the Dutch who at that time controlled the northern and richer part of Brazil. But it was on his initiative that King João sanctioned the formation of a great chartered company which, in return for a monopoly of the colony's imports, organised and armed the Portuguese convoys and so freed Brazil from the stranglehold of Dutch command of the sea. This chartered company was financed largely by Jewish capital; through thus favouring the 'New Christians', Vieira incurred the hostility of the Inquisition and some public odium, but Brazil remained Portuguese and not Dutch. The indomitable Jesuit, who, in one dramatic sermon, had even upbraided the Almighty Himself when things seemed to be going in favour of the heretics, cherished a messianic vision of a Portugal which 'has for its special end the propagation and extension of the Catholic faith in heathen lands, for which purpose God raised and founded it'. The Portuguese, he held, were destined to constitute a world empire 'conquering and subjugating all the regions of the earth under one sole empire, so that all, under the aegis of the Crown, may be gloriously placed beneath the feet of the successor of St Peter'. He even reinterpreted the old legend which held that King Sebastião, supposedly martyred in a crusade against the Moors, would one day return to his people; the prophecy, he declared after the death of his beloved monarch, referred to King João who would rise from the dead to lead his countrymen to the conquest of the world.

If Vieira belongs to the Middle Ages, or at least to the company of Christopher Columbus in his visionary obsessions, he resembles Bartolomé de las Casas in his practical and indefatigable defence of the Indians. Though he had swayed affairs of state at court and been sent on delicate diplomatic missions in Europe, he devoted many equally arduous years of his life to labouring amongst the natives, translating the Gospel into their tongues, and achieving some remarkable success in evanglisation. He campaigned vehemently against the colonists' attempts to enslave the Indian population. Rather let the whole colony perish, he declared, than live on the slave labour of the Indians;

or—a scarcely less radical alternative—let the colonists themselves turn their hands to labour, since 'it is better to live by the sweat of one's brow than by another's blood'. The colonists fought back and succeeded in blocking much of the legislation by which the Jesuit hoped to secure the Indians' protection. He was even prepared to approve the importation of Negroes from Africa as a means of saving his beloved Indians from the slavery of the plantations. Yet, when due allowance has been made for his occasional errors of judgment, his failures, and his messianic hallucinations, Antônio Vieira remains, through the force of his personality, his mastery of the literary, oratorical, and diplomatic arts, and his championship of Indians and Jews, an outstanding figure of his age who comes near to meriting his monarch's encomium as 'the greatest man in the world'.

We have noted the important part played by the Jesuits in Spanish America; in Portuguese America their role was still more notable. They provided the spiritual and intellectual cohesion for the scattered colonists, and their colleges offered the best education available in a colony where the mother country would permit no university to be founded. In many fields of scholarship and scientific investigation the Jesuit fathers produced outstanding works such as Antonil's *Cultura e Opulência do Brazil* (1711) which gives the best account of economic and social conditions during that period. But the Order still has its critics today who see in its missionary work amongst the Indians no more than a form of 'religious imperialism' which, though helping to preserve the native race, led to the destruction of its culture by imposing forms of training which were quite alien to Indian mentality. An interesting expression of contemporary reaction against the dominant role of the Jesuits may be found in what is generally accounted the finest poem to be composed during the colonial period—*O Uruguay* (1769), written shortly after the expulsion of the Order by Portugal's all-powerful Minister, the Marquis of Pombal. The author, Basílio da Gama (1741–1795), was himself a former Jesuit neophyte, and the somewhat meagre theme of his epic is the revolt of seven Indian communities allegedly incited by the Fathers to rise in protest against their proposed transfer to Portuguese sovereignty. But though anti-Jesuit, da Gama is not anti-Indian; in his descriptions of the Brazilian landscape and native life, his poem foreshadows the idealisation of the Indian and the romantic inspiration which were to characterise the work of a later generation.

Idealised Indians, of snow-white or rose-bud complexions and touching fidelity to their valiant Portuguese conqueror, also figure in another celebrated epic of the colonial period, *Caramurú* (1781) by Santa Rita Durão (1722–1784). This poem has the ambitious aim of celebrating the achievement of the Portuguese in Brazil as the great Camoens celebrated their achievement in India. It relates the exploits of the discoverer of Bahia. The first part of the poem is reminiscent of the adventures suffered in real life, by the Spaniard Cabeza de Vaca,[1] for the hero, depicted as the sole survivor of his ill-fated expedition, rises from slavery to be the acknowledged lord of the Indians who name him *Caramurú*, or Sea-dragon. He undergoes many adventures both in Europe and Brazil, and marries an Indian princess who embraces the Catholic faith and finally renounces her rights in favour of the King of Portugal, with whose blessing they live happily ever afterwards in a Brazil to which the colonists bring the benefits of Christianity and civilisation.

1. See p. 60

Basílio da Gama and Santa Rita Durão, though they lived much of their lives in Portugal, belong to the group of poets known as the School of Minas. A third member of the group was Thomaz Antônio Gonzaga (1744–1807), celebrated for his satirical no less than for his lyrical gifts. The former were directed with telling effect through the anonymous *Cartas Chilenas* (1786) against the Governor of Minas Gerais whose scandalous misrule provoked a rebellion famous in Brazilian history as the *Inconfidência Mineira*. This was suppressed and its ringleader, a dentist nicknamed 'Tiradentes' ('Toothpuller'), who had unsuccessfully tried to rouse the people by declaiming a translation of the American Declaration of Independence, was barbarously executed. Gonzaga escaped with a sentence of exile to Angola. The anguish of separation from the lover who was to have become his bride is enshrined in the lyrics of his *Marília de Dirceu* (1792) which contains some of the most moving love-poetry in the Portuguese language.

Whilst the poets of the School of Minas were engaged on their compositions and their conspiracies, Villarica de Ouro Preto, the 'Rich Town of Dark Gold', and the other settlements of the mining region were being transformed into cities whose churches are the glory of Brazil's golden age. Most famous of the artists of this period, both for the originality and fervour of his genius and for the tragedy of his life, was Antônio Francisco Lisboa (1730–1814), better known by his nickname of 'O Aleijadinho', the Little Cripple. The son of a Portuguese architect and a slave-girl, he followed brilliantly in his father's calling but was struck down at the height of his powers by a loathsome disease. Deformed and racked with pain, a misanthropic and grotesque figure with chisel and mallet strapped to his festering hands, the Little Cripple laboured on with indomitable energy for nearly three decades. He endowed the towns of Minas with matchless works of art, astonishing both in quantity and quality—elaborately carved pulpits, portals in high relief, charming medallions, designs for entire churches, and above all the moving and exquisitely carved figures of his saints, prophets, and Christs, which some critics have seen as strangely akin in spirit to the paintings of El Greco. Others again, perhaps too ready to ascribe a social and nationalist motivation to what seems to have been a triumph of the creative urge over physical deformity, claim that O Aleijadinho's masterpieces express 'a violent and daring revolt against what might be called the spirit of Portugal in Brazilian art'.

Independence and romanticism

Aleijadinho lived long enough to witness changes which were to result in emancipation from the spirit of Portugal not only in Brazil's art but in the whole of her political, economic, and cultural life. We have already noted that Napoleon's invasion of the Iberian Peninsula set in motion a train of events which gave the Spanish colonies the chance of liberating themselves by force of arms. The implications for Brazil were less violent but no less far-reaching. The Prince Regent (later to become King João VI), together with his court and government, escaped from the invaders by taking ship to Brazil. At one stroke the colony found itself the effective national territory. Rio de Janeiro, which had succeeded Bahia as the colonial capital, was transformed into a brilliant metropolis. The first newspapers, the first publishing house, the first university, public library, museum, theatre, and academy of arts made their appearance. The ports were opened to the commerce of all friendly nations.

The sudden coming of age was not unaccompanied by growing pains. The privilege of supporting a court whose lavishness threw into relief the poverty of the people had to be paid for. Whilst wealthy planters could be flattered by patents of nobility, unrest stirred the provinces. Ideas, as well as goods from abroad, circulated more freely, and the disturbing doctrines of French and English political thinkers gained currency. When the French armies withdrew from Portugal, King João decided to return to Europe and leave his son Pedro as Regent. With the backing of the wealthy planters and merchants who had no intention of seeing their country revert to its colonial status, Pedro declared the independence of Brazil. Thus, with no shedding of blood or convulsive break in continuity, political emancipation was achieved. Under the long reign of the second Emperor, the mild and scholarly Dom Pedro II, the country achieved a stability which lasted until 1889 when the constitutional monarchy in turn gave place, bloodlessly and almost imperceptibily, to the Republic.

The pattern of Brazil's history thus differs significantly from that of Spanish America. The strands are not snapped and then violently reknotted by hands which had won independence with the sword. The revulsion against the mother country is not so fierce and bitter, the repudiation of the colonial past not so complete. But if the search for a new national identity seems less vehement it is no less real. Typical of this transitional period is the figure of José Bonifácio de Andrade e Silva (1765–1838), statesman, scientist, scholar, and poet, described by Brazilians both as Father of Independence and Father of Romanticism. It was Bonifácio who, on behalf of the notables of São Paulo, penned the letter to Dom Pedro urging him to stay on in Brazil, and who also, during his later years in exile, composed verse where, for the first time in Brazilian poetry, the influence of the French and English romantics is apparent.

The appeal of Romanticism was all the greater for the emphasis it gave to those features which distinguished the New World from the Old—nature, in the exuberance and primeval grandeur of the tropics, and man, in the person of the Amerindian who inhabited it. These two sources of inspiration inform the work of the poet who best expresses this nascent spirit of Brazil—Gonçalves Dias (1823–1864). In his veins there flowed the blood of Brazil's three races, for his father was Portuguese and his mother a Negro-Indian half-breed. He was born in the Amazonian forest of the Maranhão, and though his father took him to Portugal where he received a careful education, the nostalgic memory of the tropical environment in which he was reared never left him and inspired his *Song of Exile*, possibly Brazil's most popular poem:

> Land of mine, where the palm tree grows,
> Land where the *sabia* sings. . . .

Nor was it the land alone which touched the poet's muse. Gonçalves wrote movingly, with the image of his mother before his eyes, of the slave-girl who pines for the freedom of her African home. But, above all, he sings the praises of the Indian race. If the epic poem which he wrote on the Timbiras tribe depicts them in an impossibly idealised light, as chivalrous knights or well-bred gentlemen of the forest, he devoted much of his life to serious study of aboriginal language and customs, and has left an honoured name as an ethnologist as well as being 'the first authentically Brazilian voice in poetry'.

What Gonçalves Dias accomplished for Brazilian poetry the novelist José de Alencar (1829–1877) set out to do for Brazilian prose. With the industry of a Scott or a Balzac, Alencar aimed to produce a cycle of novels which would portray the life of his people from early colonial times down to the nineteenth century, written in a style simple and vivid as the common speech of his countrymen. His best and most popular works are *O Guarani* (1857) and *Iracema* (1865). The former (which later became the subject of a popular opera) is a tale of romantic love between an Indian brave and a white girl. The theme is familiar to us from the work of the *indigenista* school in Spanish America. But if Alencar's plots seem contrived and his characters somewhat wooden, they nevertheless had enough life of their own to win enormous popularity and greatly to increase the vogue of the Indian in Brazil. The reader must not look for penetrating sociological analysis; it is enough to let himself be carried along by the story, as the Indian Peri and his white lover are carried along on their improvised raft whilst the flood-waters bear them trustingly towards a happier future.

The emancipation of the Negro

Independence from Portugal, which brought in its train this romantic cult of the Indian, was slow to affect attitudes towards the third—the African—component of the Brazilian race. If Brazil had its palm trees and its sweet song of the *sabia*, it also still had its slaves. The latter had long been deemed indispensable to the economy of the country. 'Without such slaves it is not possible to do anything in Brazil', a colonial writer had declared. 'Without them the sugar mills cannot grind, nor can the land be cultivated; for which purpose slaves are necessary and cannot be dispensed with. If anyone feels himself offended by this, his scruples will avail him nothing.' 'Let us have the honesty to recognise the fact that only a method of colonisation based upon large-scale property and upon slavery', concludes the distinguished sociologist Gilberto Freyre, 'would have been capable of surmounting the enormous obstacles in the way of the European civilisation of Brazil.' Slavery had, of course, also existed in the Spanish colonies, but it had never become basic to the society and economy as it had done in Brazil. Nor did the Brazilian slaves have the opportunity of emulating their brothers in Spanish America who volunteered for the patriot armies and reaped the reward of emancipation. Brazil's Negroes had, it is true, played a notable part in the wars against the Dutch, one of their leaders, Henrique Dias, achieving fame and later figuring as a hero in Santa Rita Durão's *Caramurú*. But Brazil knew no cult of the Noble Negro such as that popularised by Mrs Aphra Behn's *Oroonoko* in Europe in the seventeenth century.

As the nineteenth century wore on, the traditional attitude towards slavery came under the challenge of both external and internal pressures. Externally, there was the cutting off of supplies from Africa through the banning of the slave-trade, though its high-handed enforcement by the British Navy aroused more xenophobic resentment than humanitarian approval. There was also the contagious example of the abolitionist triumph in the United States after the Civil War, and a growing realisation that a slave-holding Brazil could never take the place due to her in the comity of civilised nations. The Emperor Pedro II, with his liberal sentiments and his sensitivity to currents of European thought, was particularly galled by the persistence of the hateful institution in his country, though he hesitated to move against it for fear of the economic ruin which threatened to fall upon the plantation owners. But the introduction of machinery was steadily making slavery an anachronism. Free labour, too, was proving a more efficient means of cultivating coffee, which was replacing sugar as the nation's chief source of wealth. As voluntary manumission and measures of emancipation by categories gained ground, total abolition appeared more and more within the reach of practical politics. It was finally achieved in 1888.

The triumph of the abolitionist cause was preceded by a campaign in which poets and men of letters played a notable part. Gonçalves Dias, though chiefly concerned with vindicating the Indian, had touched on the theme of slavery. Alencar, though likewise drawn to romanticising the Indian, had taken a practical step in favour of the Negroes by abolishing a notorious slave-market during his term of office as Minister of Justice. But the writer who threw himself most fervently into the cause of the slaves was Castro Alves (1847–1871). Though the life of this brilliant young poet was cut short at the age of twenty-four, the flaming verse in which he depicted the sufferings of the slaves both fascinated his readers and shocked them into an awareness of the social injustice on which their society rested. If poems such as *Voices of Africa* and *The Slave Ship* are redolent of Victor Hugo at his most colourful and grandiloquent, we are never in doubt as to their author's burning sincerity. At times his muse transcends the theme of Brazil's slaves and speaks for the down-trodden of every land and age, and of their longing for the day when men of all nations and classes will live together peacefully in a world that has become 'one vast tent for all humanity'. In such lines as these, the 'Poet of the Slaves' reveals himself as a precursor of the 'proletarian poets' of today.

If Castro Alves could do no more in his brief life than stir men's consciences with his clarion call, there were others ready to martial the forces of emancipation. The Negro and the *mulatto* came to figure more and more frequently in the verse and popular fiction of the period, generally in a romantic and sentimental light. The most widely read novel of this kind was Bernardo da Silva Guimarães' *A Escrava Isaura* (1875), the tale of a virtuous near-white *mulatto* slave-girl who surmounts all misfortunes and perils and ends by marrying a millionaire husband. Nor was it only Romanticism which made its contribution to the abolitionist cause. The Positivists also attacked slavery as incompatible with the scientific progress and human well-being in which they believed. Sílvio Romero (1851–1914), literary historian and pioneer folklorist, sang the praises of the runaway slaves of the seventeenth century who had founded and preserved for some sixty years their independent 'republic' of Palmares, herald of the future emancipation of their race, and by recording examples of negro popular verse he revealed the existence of a rich vein of folklore which later writers and composers were to turn to good account. With Joaquim Nabuco (1849–1910) and Ruy Barbosa (1848–1923) the movement found champions who fought for emancipation through political action as well as through their writings. In his *O Abolicionismo* (first published in London in 1883) Nabuco gave a classical rebuttal of the slave-owners' case, and his fascinating autobiography *Minha Formação* (1909) records the honourable part played in the abolitionist campaign by this most cultivated and cosmopolitan of Brazilians who chose elegant French Alexandrines as the vehicle for some of his denunciations. Ruy Barbosa, jurist, politician, and spokesman of pan-Americanism and the rights of the small nations, was no less eloquent in his advocacy of emancipation, as indeed of all causes to advance the twin goals of human freedom and legality. Barbosa's credo was that of the great Liberals of the nineteenth century: 'I believe in omnipotent Liberty, creator of healthy nations; I believe in Law, which is derived from it and is its chief organ, the first of its necessities.' And like Sarmiento, Alberdi, Martí, and others, Barbosa wrote his best work, his *Cartas da Inglaterra* (1896), in exile.

A curious feature of the abolitionist campaign in Brazil is that, with few exceptions, such as José do Patrocinio the *mulatto* writer (1854–1905), its leaders belonged to the white, patrician, slave-owning class. Men of Negro blood, even when fitted by education and ability to do so, seldom took a leading part in it. We are struck by this apparent paradox when we consider the work of the man who is generally acclaimed as Brazil's leading novelist, Joaquim Maria Machado de Assis (1839–1908). Born of a Negro father and a white mother in the *favelas* of Río, this brilliant *mulatto* made a name for himself as essayist, critic, poet, short-story writer, and author of a series of ironic novels—*Memórias Póstumas de Braz Cubas* (1881), *Quincas Borba* (1890), and *Dom Casmurro* (1900). Machado de Assis has been described as 'the most completely disenchanted writer in occidental literature'. He writes, as he himself puts it, 'with the pen of mirth and the ink of melancholy'. No breath from the burning controversies of the day ruffles the classic serenity of these pessimistic and penetrating studies of Brazilian upper-class life. Perhaps it is to this sense of detachment and sobriety of style that these books owe the universality of their appeal. It is not that Machado de Assis cynically condoned the slave-owning ethos of his day; he did not fail to recognise the degradation which slavery inevitably brought to the individual and to society. But to campaign for abolition had no place in his code of literary craftsmanship. Machado de Assis was the least *engagé* of writers. Here was no angry young *mulatto* inveighing against a world which denied a rightful place for himself and his kind. Though he never lost his ironic reserve and his essentially pessimistic view of human nature, Machado de Assis had little cause to complain that society had denied him personally the recognition due to his exceptional talents and his exemplary professional and domestic conduct. He received many honours during his lifetime, and his reputation has not been dimmed by the passing years. Perhaps, after all, the greatest service which he rendered to the cause of his coloured fellow citizens was to prove through the dedicated cultivation of his own genius that they had it within them to contribute to the highest manifestations of the human spirit.

This brings us to the heart of the question with which so much of Brazilian thinking has been concerned: the effect of miscegenation on the nation's character and destiny. In Spanish America, as we have seen, the cross was between European and Indian and the debate turned on the resulting *mestizo*. In Brazil the hybrid pattern is more complex, for the components are not two but three, and the differing proportions of admixture have given rise to a wide variety of physical types. Of these, it is the Negro stock and its derivatives which are most commonly taxed with inferiority. Brazil's *mulattoes*, in particular, in the words of an English traveller, 'seem to unite the vices of savage and civilised life'. The very word '*mulatto*' became a term of abuse, and in early works such as Antonil's *Cultura e Opulência do Brazil* we find already expressed a certain compassion for the Negro coupled with contempt for the *mulatto* who is commonly branded as perfidious, overbearing, arrogant, and generally depraved. The classic figure of *mulatto* treachery (in contrast to the loyal Negro symbolised by Henrique Dias) was traditionally held to be the able but unscrupulous Calabar who offered his services to the Dutch. But in time he begins to appear in a different light. In the *Calabar* of Agrário de Menezes (1834–1863) the eponymous hero of the play is shown as striving to vindicate the status of the *mulatto*, whilst Sílvio Romero regards him as the symbol of the emerging Brazilian race. Who, indeed, can be considered more authentically 'Brazilian' than the offspring of Portuguese master and coloured slave? The proverb had it that 'Brazil is a hell for blacks, a purgatory for whites, but a paradise for *mulattoes*'. Not always, however. Sometimes, as we have seen, the *mulatto* child was brought up and accepted fully with the white. But at others he was ignored and rejected. Aluízio Azevedo's novel *O Mulato* (1881) tells the story of such a lad, carefully brought up in Portugal, who returns to his native Maranhão (where the white population was traditionally less given to miscegenation and more to racial prejudice) only to be murdered when he tries to take his place amongst the whites who are culturally and morally, but not socially, his inferiors.

As the nineteenth century wore on, and the flow of slaves from Africa gave way to that of free immigrants from Europe, there were those who began to ask themselves what effect all this might have on the development of the Brazilian people. Would it invigorate the nation with an infusion of superior stock, or would it act as a dissolvent and simply increase the general degeneration? Such are the questions discussed by José Pereira de Graça Aranha (1868–1931) in his famous novel *Canaã* (1902). The book may still please through its descriptions of Brazilian landscape and customs, but the prolix philosophising of the German immigrants about this nineteenth-century Canaan carry less conviction today. Graça Aranha believed that it was the mixed blood of the Brazilian people that was the cause of their inferiority. Had not the Comte de Gobineau, creator of the myth of Nordic superiority, been an envoy at the court of Dom Pedro II and based his racial theories on his observations of Brazil? The years which followed the abolition of slavery and the establishment of the Republic proved to be a time of turmoil and disillusionment. The lot of the ex-slaves, especially when exploited by an urban proletariat, was often worse than it had been on the patriarchal planations. Banditry was rife in the provinces, and corruption ruled public life. One is reminded of the period of anarchy, abuse of power, and the feeling of having 'ploughed the sea' which afflicted the *próceres* of Spanish America's independence more than half a century earlier. And as the Spanish American thinkers had lamented that, though independent, they were still inhibited by old prejudices and ways of thought, so it appeared to many Brazilian thinkers—even those who rejected the thesis of inferiority induced by miscegenation—that the incubus of slavery still distorted men's minds.

Problems of the backlands

The year in which *Canaã* was published saw the appearance of another book which was destined to win still greater fame—*Os Sertões* by Euclides da Cunha (1866–1909). The *sertões* are the vast hinterland of hill and scrub through which the *bandeirantes* had ranged in search of Indians, gold, emeralds, or diamonds, founding settlements as they went. They produced a race of frontiersmen and miners who differed in character and social organisation from the sedentary slave-based population of the coast. Where conditions proved favourable, their communities grew into thriving cities or gained their livelihood by mining, cattle-raising, or growing coffee. Where conditions were not favourable—and this might be the case for areas thousands of square miles in extent—the sparse population of the *sertões* passed their lives in isolation, poverty, and backwardness. The *literati* of the colonial period had paid them no attention; even the poets of the School of Minas had preferred to sing of idealised Indians rather than of the more earthy heroism of the half-breeds from whose labours their cities had sprung. Nineteenth-century Brazil awoke only gradually to an awareness of the backlands. They form the subject of one of José de Alencar's cycle of novels and of one or two other books towards the end of the century. The gifted poet Olavo Bilac (1864–1918) had also left a striking picture of the restless genius of the *bandeirantes* in the four cantos of his *O Caçador de Emeraldas*. But it was not until the appearance of *Os Sertões* that the backlands received the epic treatment that was their due.

Euclides da Cunha was a remarkable mixture of poet, journalist, and scientist. Imbued, like others of his generation, with the tenets of Positivism which had given the impetus to the republican revolution, he had trained as an engineer and served for a time in the Army. But Da Cunha harboured a deep aversion to war which, in his view, 'bears the stigmata of original banditry'. This hatred was deepened into compassion for the victims of war by his experience as a reporter attached to the expeditionary force sent to crush the rebels who had defied the Republic and were holding out round Canudos, their fortress in the backlands of the north-east. Led by their half-crazed prophet Antônio the Counsellor, the rebels inflicted incredible losses on the regulars sent against them but were at length overwhelmed and annihilated. In the years which followed, Da Cunha composed his account of the campaign and pondered the causes which had led up to it. He had returned to his profession as a civil engineer, and spent his mornings supervising the construction of a bridge and his evenings writing. One thinks of the soldier-poet Ercilla penning his epic in the intervals of respite from the Araucanian wars. The wooden hut by the bridge where Da Cunha composed *Os Sertões* is revered today by his countrymen as a national shrine.

Os Sertões is a work which defies classification. Its admirers describe it as their country's 'supreme book', its bible, and its national epic. They have variously compared it to *Don Quixote, The Divine Comedy*, *The Seven Pillars of Wisdom*, and *War and Peace*. Da Cunha himself referred to it more modestly as 'this barbarous book of my youth, this monstrous poem of brutality and force'. The description calls to mind that other Latin American classic—Sarmiento's *Facundo*. Like the latter, *Os Sertões* is a blend of biography, inspired reportage, and sociological and ecological analysis. Its descriptions of the different types which make up the rude population of the backlands are as unforgettable as Sarmiento's portraits of the men of the *pampa*. But whilst the central figure of *Facundo* is a *caudillo*, behind whom there looms the dictator of a whole nation, Da Cunha's grotesque protagonist is the sinister seer whose aberrations lead a whole deluded community to its doom. Basically, it is the same clash between Barbarism and Civilisation. But for Sarmiento, barbarism is primarily the product of the brutalising environment and will disappear once the latter is modified by education, immigration, and technical progress. Da Cunha, schooled in the Positivists' creed of biological determinism, strikes a note of deeper pessimism. Like Graça Aranha, he held the now discredited view that 'an intermingling of highly diverse races is, in the majority of cases, prejudicial. . . . Miscegenation, carried to extreme, means retrogression.' Yet, so long as they moved within the primitive environment which had shaped them, the half-breeds of the backlands revealed qualities of courage, hardihood, and integrity lacking in their cousins who had had to adapt themselves to the more sophisticated culture of the allegedly civilised 'who exhibit so lamentable a degree of barbarism towards semi-barbarism'. There was, however, no turning back to the primitive stage in which the backwoodsmen still found themselves; 'we are condemned to civilisation—either we shall progress or we shall perish'. But true progress cannot be imposed—and it is this compassion which gives *Os Sertões* its perennial appeal—by the physical destruction of what is technically inferior. 'This entire campaign would be a crime, a futile and barbarous one,' Da Cunha writes, 'if we were not to take advantage of the paths opened by our artillery, by following up our cannon with a constant, stubborn, and persistent campaign of education, with the object of drawing these rude and backward fellow-countrymen of ours into the current of our times and of our national life.'

Such is the message of Euclides da Cunha; to what extent has it been heeded? The problems of the north-east have changed but little in the last six decades. The area remains one of poverty, illiteracy, and underdevelopment. The land is still scourged by droughts which periodically drive the backwoodsmen to forsake their homes and migrate in mass to the booming industrial cities and the more favoured agricultural regions of the south. From time to time bandit chiefs, cranks, and demagogues follow in the footsteps of Antônio the Counsellor and incite the desperate and superstitious peasantry to revolt. In the twenties a young officer, Luiz Carlos Prestes, proclaiming his intention of overthrowing the government and introducing a more just social order, led his column of insurgents on an astonishing five-thousand-mile march through the Brazilian hinterland from Rio Grande do Sul to the State of Bahia; but the 'Knight of Hope' then betook himself to Moscow and returned to Brazil as the representative of international Communism. In the fifties 'Peasant Leagues' began to spring up in the north-east under a leader who displayed pictures of St. Francis, Mao Tse-Tung and Fidel Castro, and assured the peasants that if Jesus Christ were alive today he would be fighting with rifle in hand in the cause of land reform. But less demagogic efforts have also been made to cope with the problems of the backlands. Vast programmes of irrigation and public works have been launched, and the soaring buildings of the new capital, Brazilia, now rise as a symbol of the belief that the backlands are also the heartland of the nation. If intractable problems still remain the nation has at least been made conscious that they exist. Euclides da Cunha's great work has left its mark on the imagination and the conscience of his countrymen. Other books, such as João Guimarães Rosa's powerful *Grande Sertão—Veredas* (1956) and Monteiro Lobato's *Urupês* (1928), centring round the tragi-comic rustic figure of Jeca Tatu, have kept public attention focussed on the same question. A whole cult of *sertanejismo* has indeed grown up, similar to that of the *gaucho* in the River Plate area, which sees in the hardy backwoodsmen the embodiment of the nation's virtues and in the still underdeveloped interior the promise of fulfilment of Brazil's destiny.

Regionalism and universality

Brazil, with problems enough of her own, was little touched by the upheaval of the First World War. But something of the contagion of the post-war ferment spread from Europe to infect her writers and artists in the early twenties. The pulsating city of São Paulo became the centre of a new mood of irreverence and experimentation to which the name *modernismo* has been attached. Brazil's *modernismo* has nothing to do with the school of this name led by Rubén Darío some decades before. The two movements indeed differ widely in aim and method. Spanish America's *modernismo* drew heavily on foreign models, and through its obsessive concern for form and style ended by enriching not only the literature of the ex-colonies but that of the mother country herself. Brazil's *modernismo* delighted in the most exuberant stylistic licence and set store on originality at all costs and the search for *brasilidade*. Mário de Andrade (1893–1945), author of a famous poem on the *Hallucinated City* and high-priest of the movement, drew up a 'cannibalistic' manifesto facetiously threatening to devour the immortals of the Brazilian literary establishment. Some of the latter, including the respected author of *Canaã*, themselves joined the ranks of the 'cannibals'. From all this effervescence and experimentation there emerged in time more serious lines of political and social protest. Some writers, like Plínio Salgado, leader of the 'Greenshirts', were attracted to Fascism; others espoused Marxism.

But Brazil was still awaiting the revelation of her true national being, the essence of that *brasilidade* which the devotees of *modernismo* were so fond of invoking but could never fully embody. In his *Retrato do Brasil* (1928) Paulo Prado attempted an acute but profoundly pessimistic analysis of his country—'the ugliest portrait which Brazil could hope to receive from one of her sons', in the author's words. Five years later there appeared Gilberto Freyre's *Casa-Grande e Senzala* (1933) which English readers know under the title of *Masters and Slaves.* This was followed by *Sobrados e Mucambos* (1936), *Ordem e Progresso* (1959), and other studies of Brazil's social history. Of *Casa-Grande e Senzala* the American scholar Frank Tannenbaum has observed that it is 'more than just a book—it marks the closing of one epoch and the beginning of another', and declares that Brazilians are now starting to realise that 'in the future, the history of their country will be divided into two parts; that before and that after Gilberto Freyre'. This is probably an overstatement; for all its fascination and importance, Freyre's work does not stand alone, and some of its features have come under increasing fire from other scholars.

In what do the originality and significance of Freyre's writings consist? The theme of *Casa-Grande e Senzala* is the origin and growth of Brazilian society, based on the great patriarchal slave-owning families and their sugar plantations in the north-east and the way they have shaped the distinctive civilisation of Brazil. The point of departure for this study is the *casa-grande* of the masters, with its adjacent *senzala*, the slave-quarters, since 'the social history of the plantation manor house is the intimate history of practically everything Brazilian; of its domestic, conjugal life, under a polygamous slave-holding regime; of the life of the child; of its Christianity reduced to a family religion and influenced by the superstitions of the slave quarters'. The *casa-grande* and the *senzala* owe their existence to special economic requirements; 'sugar production not only stifled the democratic industries represented by the trade in brazilwood and hides; it sterilised the land for the forces of diversified farming and herding for a broad expanse around the plantation. It called for an enormous number of slaves.' As time went on, there developed what Freyre calls 'zones of fraternisation between conquerors and conquered, between masters and slaves'. This resulted in a gradual fusion of cultures, a softening of the once sharply opposed economic, social, and racial forces to produce what is most characteristic in the Brazilian national character and way of life, so that one now has 'the impression that they have grown up together fraternally, and that rather than being mutually hostile by reason of their antagonisms, they supplement one another with their differences'. The outcome, Freyre claims, is 'one of the most harmonious unions of culture with nature, and of one culture with another, that the lands of this hemisphere have ever known'.

The chief factor in bringing about this fusion was the same that we have seen operating to produce the *mestizo* throughout Spanish America: the scarcity of white women. In Brazil the process of miscegenation was more thorough-going and continuous than in Spanish America for a number of reasons which Freyre adduces, such as the Portuguese colonist's natural attraction towards coloured women, coupled with the economic incentive to multiply the available slave-labour force, to 'increase the herd'. Though stressing the positive results of miscegenation, Freyre also draws attention to some deleterious effects the master-slave relationship has had on Brazilian life and character. The exercise of arbitrary power by a minority over the servile majority has, for instance, tended to produce a strain of sadism which not only characterises relations between superiors and inferiors, but those between the dominant male and the passive female, and he even claims that 'sadism on the part of the master and corresponding masochism on the part of the slave have extended beyond the sphere of sexual and domestic life and have made themselves felt throughout our history in a broader area; social and political. We think we can find it in our political life, where the dictatorial tendency has always found ready victims on which to exercise its sadistic qualities.' But whatever defects may be noted today in the national character and social relationships, they are due, Freyre is careful to stress, not to the effects of racial admixture nor to the allegedly inferior nature of the Negro component, but rather to the deleterious effects of slavery as an institution. Nabuco had made this point in declaring that it was not the Negro race *per se* that was a negative element in the national life, but 'that race reduced to slavery'. Others assert that people show an aversion to hard work in Brazil because of its former association with slave status. Paulo Prado gloomily maintains that two of the Brazilian's principal characteristics are sensuality and envy. Freyre redresses the balance by showing, with a wealth of convincing and fascinating detail that, far from being a negative element, it is precisely its Negro component that has endowed Brazil with many of its most attractive and distinctive features.

It is these features, now increasingly recognised and appreciated, which provide the stimulus for much that is original in Brazil's culture today. They inspire the prodigious musical creations of Villa-Lobos, which range from his settings of popular melodies to the ambitious endeavour of his *Bachianas brasileiras* to fuse Brazilian folk-music with the technique of

Bach. They also inspire—since the Negro has been distinguished by his humble status no less than by his rich folklore—the compassionate, proletarian canvases of Cândido Portinari (1903–1962) and the negro verse of the many-sided poet Jorge de Lima (1895–1953) who, in his moving poem *Essa Negra Fuló*, has given Brazil at least one widely acclaimed masterpiece of that genre. In prose fiction, the same inspiration has given rise to a whole galaxy of novels, written with a strong sense of social commitment and a feeling for the regional background. For Jorge Amado (1912–) it is Bahia. For others—Graciliano Ramos (1892–1953), José Américo de Almeida (1887–)—and Lins do Rego (1901–1957), it is primarily the north-east; Lins do Rego's *Sugar-Cane Cycle* can indeed be described as the fictional counterpart to Freyre's sociological researches. Others write of Amazonia, Rio Grande do Sul, or, as in the work of the popular and prolific Érico Verissimo (1905–), of the teeming life of Brazil's cities.

The work of writers such as these remains essentially regional without being merely parochial. Their novels form so many brush-strokes in building up the composite portrait of a country which, in its rich diversity, is a world in itself. Freyre has described Brazil as 'a constellation of regions . . . a well defined system of life and culture whose greatest development has come not from a planned uniformity but from a diversity built upon a basic uniformity'. Others lay more stress on its diversity than on its uniformity. 'Despite our territorial continuity,' writes Viana Moog, 'Brazil does not form a continent; we are a cultural archipelago. And this archipelago is made up of many cultural islands, all more or less autonomous.' The individuality of these regions or 'islands' may express itself in political as well as cultural terms. During the first forty years of the republic's existence two of the most powerful regions, Minas and São Paulo, reached a tacit understanding by which they virtually monopolised the political leadership of the country by alternating the Presidency between their respective candidates. This system broke down when a *Paulista* President broke the rules by nominating another *Paulista* as his successor. Minas, deeply affronted, made a compact with the state of Rio Grande do Sul, whose governor Getúlio Vargas seized power. Two years later São Paulo declared itself in revolt, and civil war broke out. São Paulo was humbled and Vargas triumphed. He ruled Brazil autocratically for a total of nearly twenty years. Though he introduced a number of important social reforms, his concept of the *Novo Estado* was too tinged with European Fascism to find general acceptance.

If Brazil has yet to find the political and social forms most suited to its own genius, the country has moved far towards the goal of discovering its own origins and defining its true national identity. Brazil has gone further along this path than any Spanish American country except Mexico. We have noted that it was a Mexican writer, Vasconcelos, who so eloquently proclaimed the virtues of miscegenation as leading to the Cosmic Race which he prophesied would one day blossom in the exuberance of a tropical world tamed for human use by modern technology. It has been left to a Brazilian, Gilberto Freyre, to show us through his researches the detailed process by which miscegenation and the action of the tropical environment have produced a hybrid race and culture already distinguished by its originality and value. Freyre and the school of contemporary thinkers and writers whom he has influenced have done much to change Brazil's own image of itself. To quote Tannenbaum once more: 'The difference between the twenties and the sixties in Brazil is that today the Brazilians have discovered themselves. They have taken a good look and like what they see. They no longer wish to be Europeans and their intellectuals no longer escape to Paris to find something to write about. They no longer describe themselves, or are so described by their own intellectuals, as a mongrel race, inferior because it consists of a mixed people. On the contrary, they find their creative freedom, their pride in the present, their confidence in the future, precisely in this fact—that they are a mixed, a universal people.' It might be added that because Brazil's image of herself is changing, so too is her conception of the part which she may play in world affairs. Brazil has always taken pride in the Western and Catholic nature of her civilisation. She is now becoming aware that her distinctive cultural and ethnical evolution link her too in a special way to the underdeveloped countries, and particularly to the emergent nations of Africa.

Bibliography

1 General works in English

Of the several comprehensive histories of Latin America available in English, Hubert Herring: *A History of Latin America* (New York, 1962) is probably the best; G. Pendle: *Latin America*, Penguin Books (London, 1963), is a useful short account.

Good general surveys of Latin American literature are A. Torres-Ríoseco: *The Epic of Latin American Literature* (London, 1942), P. Henriquez-Ureña: *Literary Currents in Hispanic America* (Harvard, 1949), E. Veríssimo: *Brazilian Literature; an Outline* (New York, 1954) and S. Putnam: *Marvelous Journey; Four Centuries of Brazilian Literature* (New York, 1948).

G. Arciniegas: *The Green Continent* (London, 1947) contains extracts from representative Latin American works.

An excellent survey of the Spanish Colonial period is M. Picón Salas: *A Cultural History of Spanish America, from Conquest to Independence* (Berkeley, 1962). W. R. Crawford deals with the work of the *pensadores* in *A Century of Latin American Thought* (Harvard, 1961) and Leopoldo Zea chiefly with nineteenth-century trends in *The Latin American Mind* (University of Oklahoma, 1963).

Interesting accounts of pre-Columbian thought, religion, and poetry in Mexico are given in M. León Portilla: *Aztec Thought and Culture* (University of Oklahoma), L. Sejourne: *Burning Water* (London, 1957), Irene Nicholson's *Firefly in the Night* (London, 1959), and J. E. Soustelle's *Daily Life under the Aztecs* (London,

1961): and for Peru, in L. Baudin: *Daily Life under the Incas* (London, 1961). An English version of the *Popol Vuh* has been made by D. Goetz and S. G. Morley (London, 1951).

2 English translations of some of the works mentioned in the text

Alegría, Ciro	*Broad and Alien is the World* Tr. by H. de Onis (New York, 1941)
Alencar, José de	*Iracema, the Honey-Lips; a Legend of Brazil* Tr. by I. Burton (London, 1886)
Amado, Jorge	*The Violent Land* Tr. by S. Putnam (New York, 1945)
Aranha, Graça	*Canaan* Tr. by M. J. Lorente (Boston, 1920)
Asturias, M. A.	*The President* Tr. by F. Partridge (London, 1963)
Azuela, Maranio	*The Underdogs* Tr. by E. Munguia (New York, 1929)
Carpentier, Alejo	*The Lost Steps* Tr. by H. de Onis (London, 1956)
Castellanos, Rosario	*The Nine Guardians* Tr. by Irene Nicholson (London, 1959)
Cunha, E. da	*Rebellion in the Backlands* Tr. by S. Putman (Chicago, 1944)
Díaz del Castillo, B.	*The Conquest of New Spain* Tr. by J. M. Cohen, Penguin Books (London, 1963)
Ercilla, Alonso de	*The Araucaniad* Tr. by C. M. Lancaster and P. T. Manchester (Nashville, 1945)
Freyre, Gilberto	*Masters and Slaves* Tr. by S. Putnam (New York, 1946)

Fuentes, Carlos — *Where the Air is Clear* (New York, 1960)
The Death of Artemio Cruz Tr. by S. Hileman (London, 1964)

Gallegos, Rómulo — *Doña Barbara* Tr. by Robert Malloy (New York, 1931)

Garcilaso de la Vega, Inca — *The Incas; Royal Commentaries* Tr. by M. Jolas from the French version of A. Gheerbrant (London, 1961)

Guimarães, Rosa J. — *The Devil to Pay in the Backlands* Tr. by J. L. Taylor and H. de Onis (New York, 1963)

Güiraldes, R. — *Don Segundo Sombra* Tr. by H. de Onis, Penguin Books (London, 1948)

Hernández, José — *Martin Fierro the Gaucho* Tr. by Walter Owen (Oxford, 1935)

Icaza, Jorge — *Huasipungo* Tr. by M. Savill (London, 1962)

Isaacs, Jorge — *María, a South American Romance* Tr. by T. A. Janvier (New York, 1925)

López y Fuentes, G. — *The Indian* Tr. by Anita Brenner (New York, 1937)

Machado de Assis — *Epitaph of a small winner* Tr. by W. L. Grossman (London, 1953)
Dom Casmurro Tr. by Helen Caldwell (London, 1953)
The Heritage of Quincas Borba Tr. by Clotilde Wilson (London, 1954)

Martí, José — *The America of José Martí* Tr. by J. de Onis (New York, 1953)

Matto de Turner, C. — *Birds without a Nest* Tr. by J. G. J. (London, 1904)

Paz, Octavio — *The Labyrinth of Solitude*
Tr. L. Kemp (New York and London, 1961)

Ramos, Graciano — *Anguish*
Tr. by L. C. Kaplan (New York, 1946)

Rivera, José Eustacio — *The Vortex*
Tr. by F. J. Stimson (New York, 1922)

Sarmiento, Domingo Faustino — *Life in the Argentine Republic in the Days of the Tyrants*
Tr. by Mrs H. Mann (New York, 1868)
A Sarmiento Anthology
Ed. by W. W. Bunkley (Princeton, 1948)

Vasconcelos, José — *A Mexican Ulysses*
Tr. by W. Rex Crawford (Indiana, 1963)

Index